BLOCKBUSTERS GOLD RUN

This book adaptation of *Blockbusters* 'Gold Run'
can be used in two ways. By yourself you can
solve the clues as you would a crossword puzzle,
writing the answers in the spaces provided and
shading or colouring in the hexagons; or, you can
play it as a game with a friend, one being the
quizmaster, and one being the competitor, trying
to get a link from left to right across the board in
sixty seconds – or however long you feel is fair.

Whether you solve the clues yourself, or with a
friend, you'll have hours of amusement and have
masses of information at your fingertips.

Also in the Blockbusters series in Sphere Books:

BLOCKBUSTERS QUIZ BOOK 1
BLOCKBUSTERS QUIZ BOOK 2
BLOCKBUSTERS QUIZ BOOK 3
BLOCKBUSTERS QUIZ BOOK 4

Blockbusters
Gold Run

**Based on the Central Independent Television series
produced in association with Mark Goodson and
Talbot Television Ltd**

SPHERE BOOKS LIMITED

First published in Great Britain by
Sphere Books Ltd 1986
27 Wrights Lane, London W8 5TZ
Copyright © 1986 by Sphere Books Ltd
Central logo copyright © 1982
Central Independent Television plc.
Central television programmes © 1983, 1984, 1985, 1986
Central Independent Television plc.
Reprinted 1986

Blockbusters Gold Run questions compiled by Colin Honnor

Sphere Books claim full responsibility for the questions
and answers in this volume and every effort has been
made to ensure their accuracy.

TRADE
MARK

Set in Times

Printed and bound in Great Britain by
Cox & Wyman Ltd, Reading

Blockbusters
Gold Run

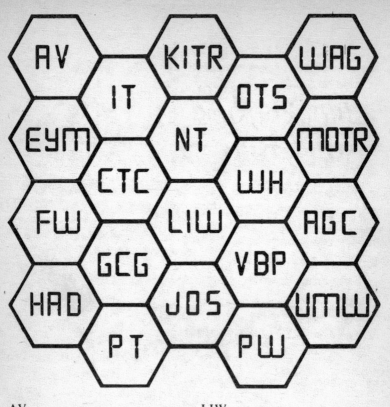

AV	————————————	LIW	————————————
EYM	————————————	JOS	————————————
FW	————————————	OTS	————————————
HAD	————————————	WH	————————————
IT	————————————	VBP	————————————
CTC	————————————	PW	————————————
GCG	————————————	WAG	————————————
PT	————————————	MOTR	————————————
KITR	————————————	AGC	————————————
NT	————————————	UMW	————————————

1

AV: What 'AV' is the explorer America is named after?

EYM: What 'EYM' is a person thought to be suitable as a husband?

FW: What 'FW' was James Joyce's last novel?

HAD: What 'HAD' is another way of saying six?

IT: What 'IT' was introduced for the first time in 1799 and is still with us?

CTC: What 'CTC' is to stop silly talk and come to the point?

GCG: What 'GCG' was a high-ranking officer who refused to leave Khartoum and was killed by the Mahdi?

PT: What 'PT' is a voyeur?

KITR: What 'KITR' is to osculate within the circle; a children's game?

NT: What 'NT' are collective names for places like Basildon, Cumbernauld and Corby?

LIW: What 'LIW' is to lurk in ambush?

JOS: What 'JOS' was a proposal to halve a baby between two women?

OTS: What 'OTS' is the place where spinsters of a certain age are said to find themselves?

WH: What 'WH' is any insensate campaign, like McCarthy's against communists in America?

VBP: What 'VBP' is to take part in an election on behalf of someone else?

PW: What 'PW' was the pretender who wasn't Lambert Simnel?

WAG: What 'WAG' is Liverpool's picture exhibition?

MOTR: What 'MOTR' is one of the titles of Lord Denning?

AGC: What 'AGC' is a form of nuclear reactor favoured by the Scottish Electricity Board?

UMW: What 'UMW' is Dylan Thomas' play for voices?

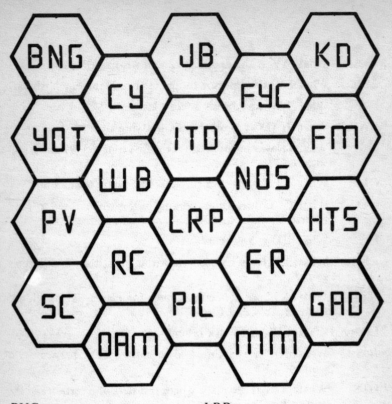

BNG	_____	LRP	_____
YOT	_____	PIL	_____
PV	_____	FYC	_____
SC	_____	NOS	_____
CY	_____	ER	_____
WB	_____	MM	_____
RC	_____	KD	_____
OAM	_____	FM	_____
JB	_____	HTS	_____
ITD	_____	GAD	_____

BNG: What 'BNG' was the uniform worn by the Confederate Army?

YOT: What 'YOT' do you blow when you boast?

PV: What 'PV' is a sweet-scented, purple-blue flower from an Italian city that's famous for ham?

SC: What 'SC' is something immune from criticism or aggression, like a holy animal?

CY: What 'CY' is a bright colour beloved by Auguste Renoir?

WB: What 'WB' were relations who flew a bi-plane for the first time at Kitty Hawk?

RC: What 'RC' did President Kennedy use to sit in to ease his back?

OAM: What 'OAM' is a term for 'of great age', like a biblical bloke?

JB: What 'JB' wrote *39 Steps* and became Lord Tweedsmuir?

ITD: What 'ITD' is the place you end up in if you fall overboard, or crash an aircraft at sea?

LRP: What 'LRP' is the grave, when you finally get there?

PIL: What 'PIL' is when you've decided to leave something on one side for the time being?

FYC: What 'FYC' is a group whose record 'Johnny' achieved some cult interest in 1985?

NOS: What 'NOS' is a tennis player thought likely to be top?

ER: What 'ER' is a Scottish dance for four couples in line?

MM: What 'MM' was the girlfriend of the outlaw of Sherwood Forest?

KD: What 'KD' sang 'Don't go breaking my heart' with Elton John?

FM: What 'FM' is the highest rank of army officer?

HTS: What 'HTS' is the call to crew before departure of merchant vessels?

GAD: What 'GAD' is the revived Damon Runyan musical?

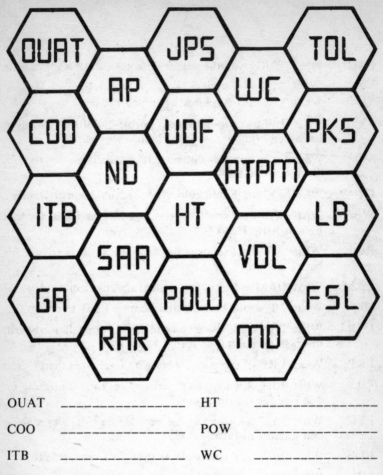

OUAT	_____	HT	_____
COO	_____	POW	_____
ITB	_____	WC	_____
GA	_____	ATPM	_____
AP	_____	VDL	_____
ND	_____	MD	_____
SAA	_____	TOL	_____
RAR	_____	PKS	_____
JPS	_____	LB	_____
UDF	_____	FSL	_____

OUAT: What 'OUAT' is how fairy stories ought to begin?

COO: What 'COO' is the critical atmosphere; what people think at the moment?

ITB: What 'ITB' is if you are dotty, potty or barmy; this is where you have bats?

GA: What 'GA' is a contract without legal force that will be fulfilled as a matter of honour?

AP: What 'AP' built his grotto of seashells in Twickenham?

ND: What 'ND' is a person who thinks it impressive to mention famous acquaintances all the time?

SAA: What 'SAA' is the tall, thin knight in *Twelfth Night*?

RAR: What 'RAR' is perfectly OK, like a wet day in a drought?

JPS: What 'JPS' was the philosopher who, with Simone de Beauvoir, made existentialism a Big Thing?

UDF: What 'UDF' is the Irish Citizen Army?

HT: What 'HT' is the altoist with 'Air' and with a sextet?

POW: What 'POW' was an inmate of a war camp?

WC: What 'WC' was War Correspondent for the *Morning Post* during the Boer War – among other things?

ATPM: What 'ATPM' is a film based on the Watergate story?

VDL: What 'VDL' was a Dutchman's name originally given to Tasmania?

MD: What 'MD' is September 29th?

TOL: What 'TOL' was the one that didn't have the Fruit of Knowledge on it?

PKS: What 'PKS' is the forensic pathologist who wrote *40 Years of Murder*?

LB: What 'LB' won the *Daily Mail* prize for flying the Channel in 1909?

FSL: What 'FSL' is professional chief of the British Navy?

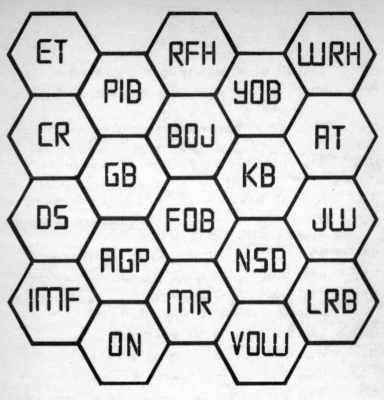

ET	_____	FOB	_____
CR	_____	MR	_____
DS	_____	YOB	_____
IMF	_____	KB	_____
PIB	_____	NSD	_____
GB	_____	VOW	_____
AGP	_____	WRH	_____
ON	_____	AT	_____
RFH	_____	JW	_____
BOJ	_____	LRB	_____

ET: What 'ET' was Velvet who won The National?

CR: What 'CR' wanted the British to be in control from Cape to Cairo?

DS: What 'DS' is also known as Sirius or Alpha Canis Majoris?

IMF: What 'IMF' is the World Financial Organisation?

PIB: What 'PIB' is a pantomime about a cat?

GB: What 'GB' is among the largest and fiercest carnivores of North America?

AGP: What 'AGP' is one of the wonderful landmarks in Egypt?

ON: What 'ON' is the devil in elderly form?

RFH: What 'RFH' is the South Bank musical venue?

BOJ: What 'BOJ' was where Jellicoe was inconclusively in command in May 1916?

FOB: What 'FOB' is in high spirits, or having eaten pulses?

MR: What 'MR' composed *Bolero*?

YOB: What 'YOB' do you get when you are revenged?

KB: What 'KB' acts in *Duty Free* and has a Cornish restaurant?

NSD: What 'NSD' is not to speak of expiring?

VOW: What 'VOW' is Goldsmith's famous novel about a parson?

WRH: What 'WRH' was the original chief character in *Citizen Kane*?

AT: What 'AT' is the greatest conductor of the NBC Symphony Orchestra and probably in the world?

JW: What 'JW' pioneered Neo-Classical China with white figures on a blue background?

LRB: What 'LRB' is the famous small publication by Mao Tse-tung?

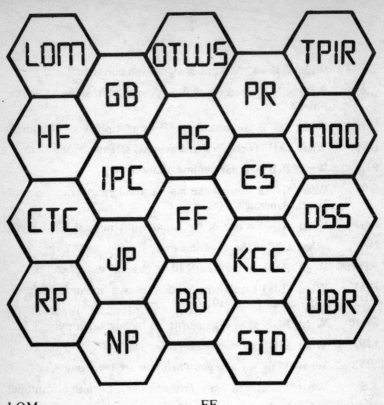

LOM	_____	FF	_____
HF	_____	BO	_____
CTC	_____	PR	_____
RP	_____	ES	_____
GB	_____	KCC	_____
IPC	_____	STD	_____
JP	_____	TPIR	_____
NP	_____	MOO	_____
OTWS	_____	DSS	_____
AS	_____	UBR	_____

LOM: What 'LOM' is a kind of sleeve or cut of meat?

HF: What 'HF' introduced the assembly line into car manufacture?

CTC: What 'CTC' is dancing very close; not done now?

RP: What 'RP' is used for flattening pastry and erring husbands?

GB: What 'GB' is a television set?

IPC: What 'IPC' is an established magazine group?

JP: What 'JP' was the man who was once Argentina's president?

NP: What 'NP' is what you are said to be as neat as?

OTWS: What 'OTWS' means you are bad-tempered, and this is how you get out of bed?

AS: What 'AS' is the doyen of players of the Spanish guitar?

FF: What 'FF' is a scaled creature that can get airborne?'

BO: What 'BO' is a sporting competition won five times by Peter Thomson?

PR: What 'PR' is a system of Parliamentary voting favoured by the Liberals?

ES: What 'ES' is the name for magnesium sulphate as a purgative?

KCC: What 'KCC' is in Cambridge, where nine Lessons and Carols are sung each Christmas?

STD: What 'STD' means to come to a compromise by division of the remainder?

TPIR: What 'TPIR' is hosted by Leslie Crowther?

MOO: What 'MOO' is Joan of Arc's nickname because of the town she relieved?

DSS: What 'DSS' are Hebrew and Aramaic manuscripts stored in a cave near Qumran?

UBR: What 'UBR', the 130th of which was delayed, took place on Sunday March 18th 1984?

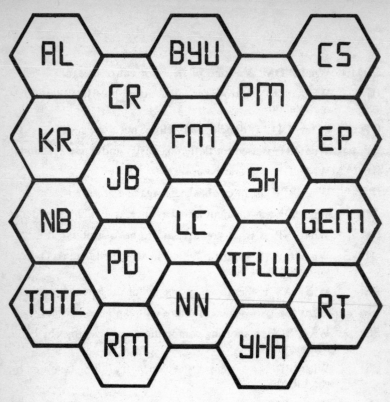

AL	_____	LC	_____
KR	_____	NN	_____
NB	_____	PM	_____
TOTC	_____	SH	_____
CR	_____	TFLW	_____
JB	_____	YHA	_____
PD	_____	CS	_____
RM	_____	EP	_____
BYU	_____	GEM	_____
FM	_____	RT	_____

AL: Which 'AL' was an American President killed in the theatre?

KR: What 'KR' is a phrase used at the end of an informal letter?

NB: What 'NB', born in Corsica, died in St Helena?

TOTC: What 'TOTC' was Dickens' novel set against the background of the French Revolution?

CR: What 'CR' is the Ecclesiastical Head of the United Synagogue in Great Britain?

JB: What 'JB' are edible infants?

PD: What 'PD' is said of boxers suffering from brain damage due to constant blows?

RM: What 'RM' are off-the-peg clothes, not to customers' own measurements?

BYU: What 'BYU' is Uncle Robert telling me 'All will be well'?

FM: What 'FM' means not quite right in the head?

LC: What 'LC' do printers call the small letters?

NN: What 'NN' is the Charles Dickens' novel in which Smike is a central character?

PM: What 'PM' is the impossible system to provide unceasing movement?

SH: What 'SH' is the detective who first appears in *A Study in Scarlet*?

TFLW: What 'TFLW' is the film for which Jeremy Irons won the Variety Club's Best Actor Award?

YHA: What 'YHA' is cheap accommodation for hikers who belong?

CS: What 'CS' is the famous clipper in dry dock at Greenwich?

EP: What 'EP' is the finished article as opposed to raw material?

GEM: What 'GEM' is the strange looking creature that jealousy is described as in Shakespeare's *Othello*?

RT: What 'RT' is a colloquial phrase for the garment business?

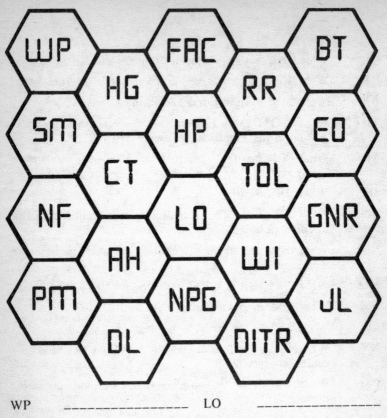

WP	_____	LO	_____
SM	_____	NPG	_____
NF	_____	RR	_____
PM	_____	TOL	_____
HG	_____	WI	_____
CT	_____	DITR	_____
AH	_____	BT	_____
DL	_____	EO	_____
FAC	_____	GNR	_____
HP	_____	JL	_____

WP: What 'WP' became Prime Minister at the age of twenty-four?

SM: What 'SM' is a novel written by Mary Ann Evans under a pseudonym?

NF: What 'NF' is the home of small, hardy, half-wild ponies in Southern England?

PM: What 'PM' is an NCO commanding regimental bagpipes?

HG: What 'HG' was the object of quest for Arthurian Knights?

CT: What 'CT' is a type of story that contains warnings and morals?

AH: What 'AH' was the maker of the thriller called *Strangers on a Train*?

DL: What 'DL' was the Scottish missionary who was finally found at Ujiji?

FAC: What 'FAC' is England's national take-away food?

HP: What 'HP' is author of *The Caretaker*, and husband of Antonia Fraser?

LO: What 'LO' means to omit?

NPG: What 'NPG' is a collection of pictures of notable Britons, in St Martin's Lane?

RR: What 'RR' is the ecclesiastical prefix for designating a bishop?

TOL: What 'TOL' had the white part of it originally built for William the Conqueror?

WI: What 'WI' is the organisation for the benefit of rural females?

DITR: What 'DITR' is a sharp nudge in the midriff?

BT: What 'BT' was author of farces, including *Rookery Nook*?

EO: What 'EO' is something astonishing, a revealing event?

GNR: What 'GNR' goes from London towards Scotland as the A1?

JL: What 'JL' was the famous black boxer called The Brown Bomber?

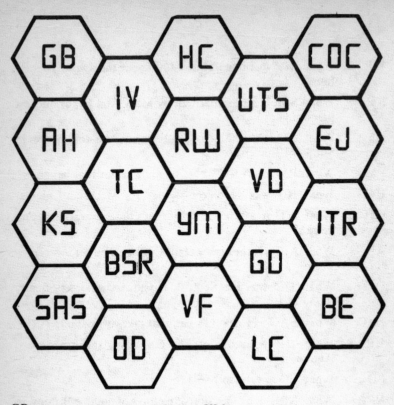

GB _____   YM   _____

AH _____   VF   _____

KS _____   UTS _____

SAS _____   VD   _____

IV _____   GD   _____

TC _____   LC   _____

BSR _____   COC _____

OD _____   EJ   _____

HC _____   ITR _____

RW _____   BE   _____

GB: What 'GB' is a band of open country round a city?

AH: What 'AH' was the author who wrote *Brave New World*?

KS: What 'KS' was the nuclear worker who was killed in a car accident, played by Meryl Streep?

SAS: What 'SAS' is football with an odd, small-sounding team?

IV: What 'IV' means without success?

TC: What 'TC' means successive united hurrahs?

BSR: What 'BSR' were precursors of the force introduced by Sir Robert Peel?

OD: What 'OD' is an illness like silicosis, caused by a person's work?

HC: What 'HC' is a tree that produces conkers?

RW: What 'RW' was the revolutionary composer who spent his last years at Bayreuth?

YM: What 'YM' is a famous church damaged by lightning in July 1984?

VF: What 'VF' is the novel by Thackeray in which Becky Sharp is the heroine?

UTS: What 'UTS' is a phrase that sounds the opposite but means the same as down the drain?

VD: What 'VD' is February 14th?

GD: What 'GD' is the American apple now grown in France and derided in Britain?

LC: What 'LC' is the army officer in command of a regiment?

COC: What 'COC' is the offence against the authority of a Judge?

EJ: What 'EJ' sang goodbye to the Yellow Brick Road?

ITR: What 'ITR' means being overdrawn at the bank?

BE: What 'BE' is a phrase that means to make neither profit or loss?

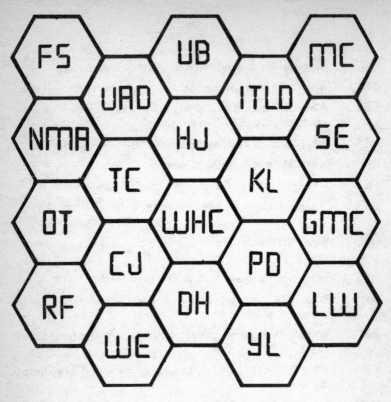

FS	_____	WHC	_____
NMA	_____	DH	_____
OT	_____	ITLD	_____
RF	_____	KL	_____
UAD	_____	PD	_____
TC	_____	YL	_____
CJ	_____	MC	_____
WE	_____	SE	_____
UB	_____	GMC	_____
HJ	_____	LW	_____

FS: What 'FS' is a naval vessel carrying an admiral?

NMA: What 'NMA', formed in February 1645, won the English Civil War?

OT: What 'OT' is a room in a hospital reserved for surgery?

RF: What 'RF' is a tropical jungle?

UAD: What 'UAD' means alternating good and bad patches of luck?

TC: What 'TC' is the popular name for the University of Dublin?

CJ: What 'CJ' is Britain's busiest station – found in South London?

WE: What 'WE' means an unwanted gift?

UB: What 'UB' is the dole?

HJ: What 'HJ' is an athletic competition in which you leap over a bar?

WHC: What 'WHC' is the title won by Jersey Joe Walcott?

DH: What 'DH' was Chancellor of The Exchequer for Labour from 1974 to 1979?

ITLD: What 'ITLD' was where David found himself?

KL: What 'KL' was the legendary monarch who had daughters called Regan, Goneril and Cordelia?

PD: What 'PD' is Wiltshire's special Pathogens Laboratory?

YL: What 'YL' is a lump of wood burnt on Christmas Eve?

MC: What 'MC' did many of his stunts in *Some Mothers Do Have 'Em*?

SE: What 'SE' is an Andrew Lloyd Webber show?

GMC: What 'GMC' is the body that regulates the right to practise as a doctor in the UK?

LW: What 'LW' are all Socialists, more or less?

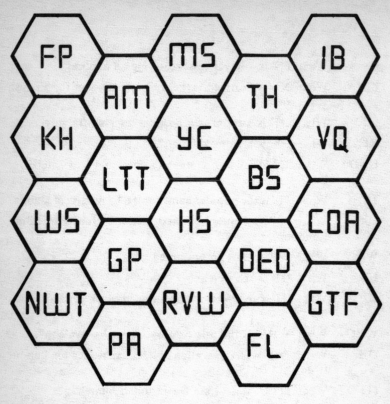

FP	_____	HS	_____
KH	_____	RVW	_____
WS	_____	TH	_____
NWT	_____	BS	_____
AM	_____	DED	_____
LTT	_____	FL	_____
GP	_____	IB	_____
PA	_____	VQ	_____
MS	_____	COA	_____
YC	_____	GTF	_____

FP: What 'FP' was the youngest man to win the world heavyweight title?

KH: What 'KH' played opposite Jane Fonda's father in his last film?

WS: What 'WS' is a painted burial place or metaphorically a hypocrite?

NWT: What 'NWT' is part of coldest Canada?

AM: What 'AM' was the convict father of Estelle in *Great Expectations*?

LTT: What 'LTT' sang for his supper?

GP: What 'GP' was succeeded by the 1666 Fire of London?

PA: What 'PA' is treatment of the mind, associated with a Liberal MP's grandfather?

MS: What 'MS' means encouragement given by taking someone's side in matters of opinion?

YC: What 'YC' is shown to a soccer player when he's getting a caution?

HS: What 'HS' is a gas that smells of bad eggs?

RVW: What 'RVW' was once the grand old man of English music?

TH: What 'TH' is an overture by Mendelssohn about Scotland, sometimes called Fingal's Cave?

BS: What 'BS' invented Dracula?

DED: What 'DED' destroyed thousands of trees in Europe?

FL: What 'FL' might be translated as Dirty Money?

IB: What 'IB' is a famous England cricket captain?

VQ: What 'VQ' means a much disputed or discussed point?

COA: What 'COA' is a device in heraldry containing a family's armorial bearing?

GTF: What 'GTF' is the first person of the Trinity?

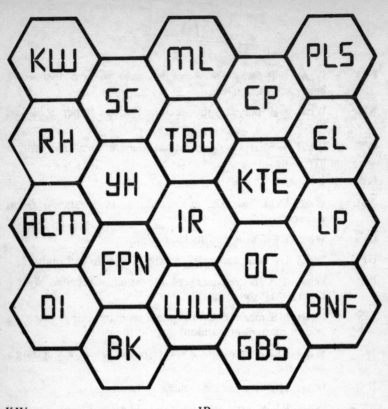

KW	_____	IR	_____
RH	_____	WW	_____
ACM	_____	CP	_____
DI	_____	KTE	_____
SC	_____	OC	_____
YH	_____	GBS	_____
FPN	_____	PLS	_____
BK	_____	EL	_____
ML	_____	LP	_____
TBO	_____	BNF	_____

KW: What 'KW' is the composer of the *Threepenny Opera*?

RH: What 'RH' is the time at which traffic is busiest?

ACM: What 'ACM' is the RAF equivalent of an admiral or a general?

DI: What 'DI' is solid carbon dioxide?

SC: What 'SC' was the man who founded the shipping line that bore his name?

YH: What 'YH' is a hedgerow bird that sings 'a little bit of bread and no cheese'?

FPN: What 'FPN' is the paper money worth five hundred pence?

BK: What 'BK' is an affectionate greeting with the eyelashes?

ML: What 'ML' is the title of a work by George Meredith and of a David Bowie number?

TBO: What 'TBO' is a theatrical event that made Rich gay, and Gay rich?

IR: What 'IR' is a cream for the skin to discourage mosquitoes from biting you?

WW: What 'WW' was a Scottish national hero, executed in 1305?

CP: What 'CP' is a bird used to take messages?

KTE: What 'KTE' was the trip in 1947 from Peru to Tuamotu?

OC: What 'OC' means not quite well – pale perhaps?

GBS: What 'GBS' wrote *Man and Superman*?

PLS: What 'PLS' means crowded together like small tinned fish?

EL: What 'EL' wrote *The Owl and the Pussycat*?

LP: What 'LP' won the Derby for the ninth time on 'Teenoso'?

BNF: What 'BNF' is in charge of Sellafield?

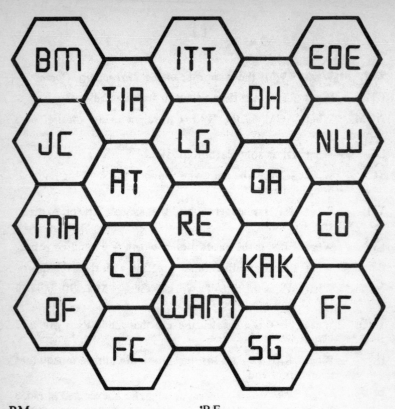

BM	_____	'RE	_____
JC	_____	WAM	_____
MA	_____	DH	_____
OF	_____	GA	_____
TIA	_____	KAK	_____
AT	_____	SG	_____
CD	_____	EOE	_____
FC	_____	NW	_____
ITT	_____	CO	_____
LG	_____	FF	_____

BM: What 'BM' is a double saucepan, like a glue pot?

JC: What 'JC' was a Polish born writer of sea-faring novels in English?

MA: What 'MA' said 'Friends, Romans and countrymen, lend me your ears'?

OF: What 'OF' is a onetime sweetheart who was once hot stuff?

TIA: What 'TIA' is a sequence of famous pictures by Hogarth depicting a lazy young learner?

AT: What 'AT' means a liking gained by experience?

CD: What 'CD' revolutionised fashion with the New Look, The Sack, and the H Line?

FC: What 'FC' is the name for LHASA in Tibet because foreigners are kept out?

ITT: What 'ITT' was first Czar of Russia, who killed his own son?

LG: What 'LG' is a very small receptacle for sweet, strong drink?

RE: What 'RE' was the territory established by Augustus in 27 BC?

WAM: What 'WAM' are the methods or systems by which a purpose can be accomplished; sometimes meaning money?

DH: What 'DH' was a notorious Dickensian school in Yorkshire?

GA: What 'GA' is the name of the mountain sometimes called K2?

KAK: What 'KAK' are one's own people, family and friends?

SG: What 'SG' is the place in the House of Commons where visitors can watch debates?

EOE: What 'EOE' is Charles Lamb's most famous solo work?

NW: What 'NW' means The Americas – especially to Dvořák?

CO: What 'CO' was leaked from the *Torrey Canyon* off Land's End?

FF: What 'FF' is the so-called 'Apple' that got us all into trouble?

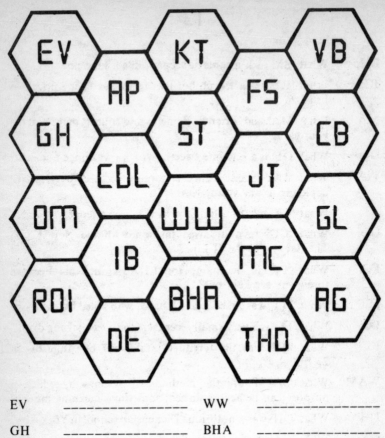

EV	_____	WW	_____
GH	_____	BHA	_____
OM	_____	FS	_____
ROI	_____	JT	_____
AP	_____	MC	_____
CDL	_____	THD	_____
IB	_____	VB	_____
DE	_____	CB	_____
KT	_____	GL	_____
ST	_____	AG	_____

EV: What 'EV' is a speed of at least 29,000 km per hour?

GH: What 'GH' is the composer of *The Planets*?

OM: What 'OM' is an elderly spinster or a card game?

ROI: What 'ROI' is a part of Europe where they still drive on the left?

AP: What 'AP' is a way of making pictures, popularised by Jackson Pollock?

CDL: What 'CDL' is an epithet or name for Richard the First?

IB: What 'IB' is a domestic article on which clothes are pressed?

DE: What 'DE' is a jazz pianist and composer whose band made 'Mood Indigo' world famous?

KT: What 'KT' means to dispose of leisure with idle pursuits?

ST: What 'ST' is the preferred acting partner of Katherine Hepburn?

WW: What 'WW' is the reference book of contemporary biography?

BHA: What 'BHA' is Murdoch's partner and Anthea's father?

FS: What 'FS' is the original UFO?

JT: What 'JT' is the English pioneer of the seed-drill – or a pop group?

MC: What 'MC' now has more inhabitants than Tokyo?

THD: What 'THD' was the period between Elba and Waterloo?

VB: What 'VB' is the flying mammal that sucks blood?

CB: What 'CB' was the girl who had a hit with 'Anyone Who Had a Heart'?

GL: What 'GL' is the economist's law that says 'bad money drives out good'?

AG: What 'AG' plays eight roles in *Kind Hearts and Coronets*?

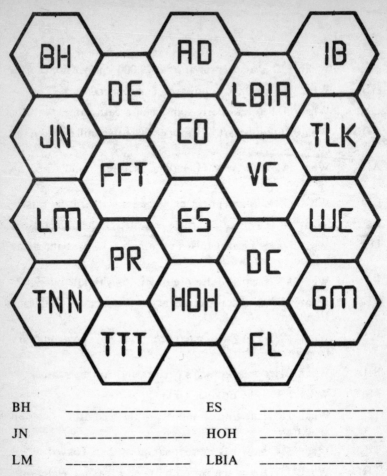

BH	_____	ES	_____
JN	_____	HOH	_____
LM	_____	LBIA	_____
TNN	_____	VC	_____
DE	_____	DC	_____
FFT	_____	FL	_____
PR	_____	IB	_____
TTT	_____	TLK	_____
AD	_____	WC	_____
CO	_____	GM	_____

BH: What 'BH' is either sent by messenger, or else not done on a machine?

JN: What 'JN' was the first premier of Tanzania?

LM: What 'LM' is a machine for cutting grass?

TNN: What 'TNN' were the years at the end of the 1800s thought to be wicked but jolly?

DE: What 'DE' was the comic whose catch phrase was 'Ooh you are awful but I like you'?

FFT: What 'FFT' is nourishment for cogitation?

PR: What 'PR' is the title sometimes given to a sovereign's eldest daughter?

TTT: What 'TTT' had love on their side in 1983?

AD: What 'AD' was a clever young scoundrel, originally in *Oliver Twist*?

CO: What 'CO' means to unmoor, or to finish a piece of knitting?

ES: What 'ES' is a new name for what was once called geography?

HOH: What 'HOH' means rather deaf?

LBIA: What 'LBIA' is Osborne's most famous play?

VC: What 'VC' is a suction apparatus for cleaning carpets?

DC: What 'DC' means bravery induced by drink?

FL: What 'FL' was the Abbé famous for Hungarian Rhapsody?

IB: What 'IB' was the world's first river crossing in Coalbrookdale designed by Abraham Darby?

TLK: What 'TLK' is the film in which Alec Guinness plans to murder his landlady?

WC: What 'WC' was the father of printing in England?

GM: What 'GM' is rubella, a danger to young, pregnant women?

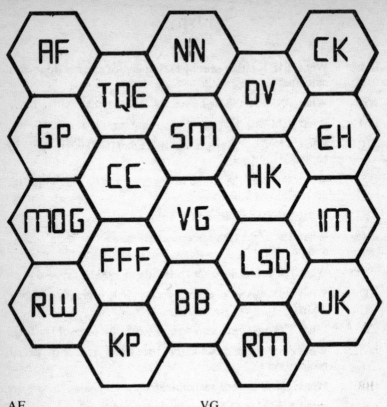

AF	_____	VG	_____
GP	_____	BB	_____
MOG	_____	DV	_____
RW	_____	HK	_____
TQE	_____	LSD	_____
CC	_____	RM	_____
FFF	_____	CK	_____
KP	_____	EH	_____
NN	_____	IM	_____
SM	_____	JK	_____

AF: What 'AF' is someone whose leg is pulled on the first of the fourth?

GP: What 'GP' is a report of proposals to which the Government is not yet committed?

MOG: What 'MOG' was a shameful assassination of Macdonalds in a valley?

RW: What 'RW' was always regarded as our first Prime Minister?

TQE: What 'TQE' means to decide to give evidence for the prosecution against accomplices?

CC: What 'CC' is kaolin, used in making porcelain?

FFF: What 'FFF' is where thy father lies, with pearls for eyes?

KP: What 'KP' is the way through the mountains that leads to Afghanistan?

NN: What 'NN' was the onetime name of the Russian town now called Gorky?

SM: What 'SM' is Warren Beatty's famous sister?

VG: What 'VG' is help in choosing a possible career?

BB: What 'BB' is between a north-east Canadian island and Greenland?

DV: What 'DV' means God willing or permitting?

HK: What 'HK' is leader of the German Christian Democrats?

LSD: What 'LSD' is something that makes work easier?

RM: What 'RM' was England's first Labour Prime Minister?

CK: What 'CK' wrote *The Water Babies*?

EH: What 'EH' do greyhounds race after?

IM: What 'IM' was sparked off by grease on ammunition in 1857?

JK: What 'JK' once had a hit with 'Everyone's Gone to the Moon' and now reports on the New York pop scene?

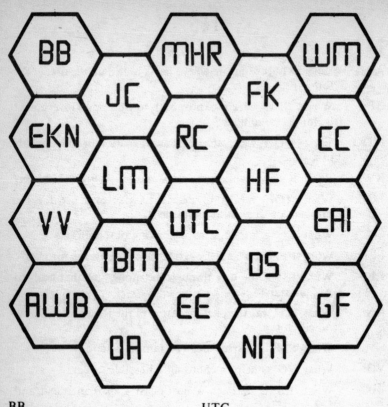

BB	_____	UTC	_____
EKN	_____	EE	_____
VV	_____	FK	_____
AWB	_____	HF	_____
JC	_____	DS	_____
LM	_____	NM	_____
TBM	_____	WM	_____
OA	_____	CC	_____
MHR	_____	EAI	_____
RC	_____	GF	_____

BB: What 'BB' means in prison?

EKN: What 'EKN' is the Mozart work for strings whose English name is 'A Little Night Music'?

VV: What 'VV' means the other way round?

AWB: What 'AWB' was once the youngest MP and is now known as TB?

JC: What 'JC' is the name of the King of Spain?

LM: What 'LM' took the song 'Wanderin' Star' to number 1 in 1970?

TBM: What 'TBM' were unfortunate rodents who lost their tails to a farmer's wife?

OA: What 'OA' is the Argentine footballer acquired by Spurs?

MHR: What 'MHR' is a conventional birthday wish?

RC: What 'RC' means manipulation from a distance?

UTC: What 'UTC' is Harriet Beecher Stowe's anti-slavery book?

EE: What 'EE' composed 'Enigma Variations'?

FK: What 'FK' is where the USA keeps its bullion?

HF: What 'HF' means clumsy: as if one's hands were pig's legs?

DS: What 'DS' is a way of classifying books?

NM: What 'NM' means limited in outlook and often prudish as well?

WM: What 'WM' was an arts and crafts pioneer who founded the Kelmscott Press?

CC: What 'CC' first landed at Botany Bay in 1770?

EAI: What 'EAI' is a McCartney and Wonder song that sounds like a piano keyboard?

GF: What 'GF' is a valuable instrument played by James Galway?

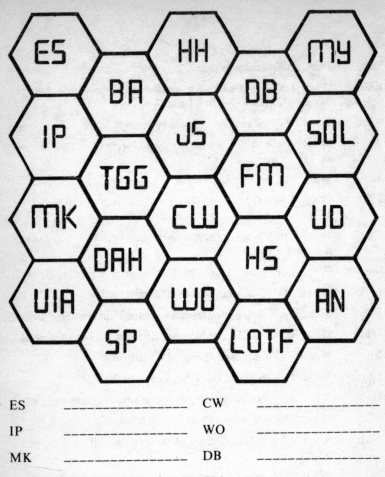

ES ————————   CW ————————

IP ————————   WO ————————

MK ————————   DB ————————

UIA ————————   FM ————————

BA ————————   HS ————————

TGG ————————   LOTF ————————

DAH ————————   MY ————————

SP ————————   SOL ————————

HH ————————   UD ————————

JS ————————   AN ————————

ES: What 'ES' was the poetic sister of Osbert and Sacheverell?

IP: What 'IP' is the part of the hand that longs for money?

MK: What 'MK' is the German title of Hitler's book about his life?

UIA: What 'UIA' means angry, militant and protesting?

BA: What 'BA' is the nickname of the proceedings that made Judge Jeffreys famous?

TGG: What 'TGG' is the novel about a bootlegger, by F. Scott Fitzgerald?

DAH: What 'DAH' means so poor that you can't afford to have your shoes repaired?

SP: What 'SP' was England's most celebrated diarist?

HH: What 'HH' means to travel by getting lifts from cars and lorries?

JS: What 'JS' is bargain time in the big stores at the beginning of the year?

CW: What 'CW' planned to rebuild London after the Great Fire of 1666?

WO: What 'WO' do you sow in a misspent youth?

DB: What 'DB' is sometimes called 'the remains'?

FM: What 'FM' is someone who brings up a child not her own?

HS: What 'HS' is the tomb outside Jerusalem in which the body of Jesus was placed?

LOTF: What 'LOTF' is the sinister story about stranded schoolboys on an island?

MY: What 'MY' are five Birmingham schoolboys who made it to number 1?

SOL: What 'SOL' holds a torch outside New York?

UD: What 'UD' grew up to be a swan?

AN: What 'AN' are stories told over a long period as entertainments for a sultan?

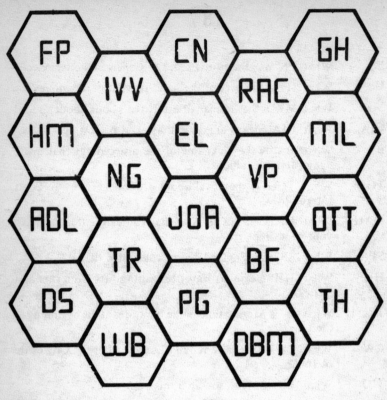

FP   _____   JOA   _____

HM   _____   PG   _____

ADL   _____   RAC   _____

DS   _____   VP   _____

IVV   _____   BF   _____

NG   _____   DBM   _____

TR   _____   GH   _____

WB   _____   ML   _____

CN   _____   OTT   _____

EL   _____   TH   _____

FP: What 'FP' is a pile of wood for burning a corpse in antiquity or in parts of Asia?

HM: What 'HM' is the French wife of King Charles the First?

ADL: What 'ADL' means a life of misery associated with canines?

DS: What 'DS' was a pupil of Glazunov who composed a Seventh Symphony known as 'The Leningrad'?

IVV: What 'IVV' is the Latin phrase meaning that you blurt out the truth when drunk?

NG: What 'NG' is mostly methane and often found with petroleum?

TR: What 'TR' is the name for the German State under Hitler?

WB: What 'WB' is the star turned director who won an Oscar for *Reds*?

CN: What 'CN' is the stone spike from Egypt that's no good for sewing?

EL: What 'EL' is the most cherished possession in the form of a young female sheep?

JOA: What 'JOA' was born at Dom Remy in about 1412?

PG: What 'PG' is the landlocked sea behind the Strait of Hormuz?

RAC: What 'RAC' means loaded with money like a King of Lydia?

VP: What 'VP' is a favourable position for viewing an event, or a situation?

BF: What 'BF' invented the lightning conductor?

DBM: What 'DBM' means the verdict of killing by accident?

GH: What 'GH' means money given on retirement or redundancy?

ML: What 'ML' is the emblem of Canada?

OTT: What 'OTT' means walking quietly and surreptitiously?

TH: What 'TH' was a fearful Greek wooden gift?

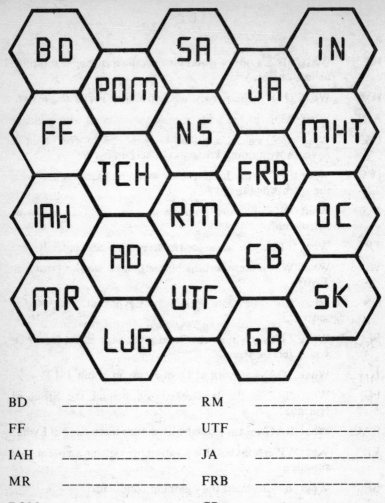

BD	_____	RM	_____
FF	_____	UTF	_____
IAH	_____	JA	_____
MR	_____	FRB	_____
POM	_____	CB	_____
TCH	_____	GB	_____
AD	_____	IN	_____
LJG	_____	MHT	_____
SA	_____	OC	_____
NS	_____	SK	_____

BD: What 'BD' means completely dessicated, like an old skeleton?

FF: What 'FF' is part of a parachute jump before the chute opens?

IAH: What 'IAH' is where Ernest Worthing was found?

MR: What 'MR' is the country singer whose big hit was 'El Paso'?

POM: What 'POM' means quick thinking in an emergency?

TCH: What 'TCH' is triangular headgear, and a ballet by De Falla?

AD: What 'AD' was the French army officer convicted in 1894 and only finally exonerated in 1930?

LJG: What 'LJG' was the Nine Days' Queen?

SA: What 'SA' is the country whose Minister for Oil is Sheik Yamani?

NS: What 'NS' is the proper name of most Christmas trees?

RM: What 'RM' is the title and form of address to the Superior of a convent?

UTF: What 'UTF' is the famous Romantic novel by Ouida?

JA: What 'JA' was one of the Railway Children and also went walkabout?

FRB: What 'FRB' is modern, and right beside a famous nineteenth century railway bridge?

CB: What 'CB' is the clavicle: a bone that riders often break?

GB: What 'GB' achieved the highest batting average in England in 1979?

IN: What 'IN' is seen with his telescope on the back of the old one pound note?

MHT: What 'MHT' is where Alice watched weird goings on with the Dormouse?

OC: What 'OC' was the Parliamentary leader who wanted his portrait to show warts and all?

SK: What 'SK' is the country whose capital is Seoul?

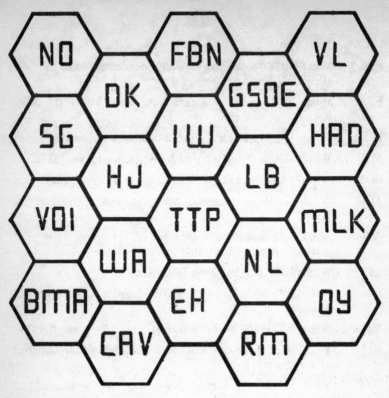

NO	_____	TTP	_____
SG	_____	EH	_____
VOI	_____	GSOE	_____
BMA	_____	LB	_____
DK	_____	NL	_____
HJ	_____	RM	_____
WA	_____	VL	_____
CAV	_____	HAD	_____
FBN	_____	MLK	_____
IW	_____	OY	_____

NO: What 'NO' is sometimes called the Cradle of Jazz?

SG: What 'SG' is the contents of a church window?

VOI: What 'VOI' was Mountbatten the last of?

BMA: What 'BMA' is the governing body for doctors?

DK: What 'DK' is the actress who often plays opposite Woody Allen?

HJ: What 'HJ' is a coat meant for riding?

WA: What 'WA' is the name given to termites because they are social insects and of pale colour?

CAV: What 'CAV' means an exact reference, originally to the Bible?

FBN: What 'FBN' is someone who decamps in the dark?

IW: What 'IW' is the pre-Roman trackway from Wiltshire to Norfolk?

TTP: What 'TTP' is a solemn engagement to give up drink?

EH: What 'EH' sang with Bob Dylan on 'Desire'?

GSOE: What 'GSOE' did Barnum call his circus?

LB: What 'LB' is the opera by Puccini based on Parisian artists' lives?

NL: What 'NL' is another name for aurora borealis?

RM: What 'RM' is where the money really comes from?

VL: What 'VL' returned to Russia from Switzerland in 1917 in a sealed train?

HAD: What 'HAD' means up out of the water and stranded?

MLK: What 'MLK' was an assassinated black religious leader in the USA?

OY: What 'OY' was a hit for the Flying Pickets?

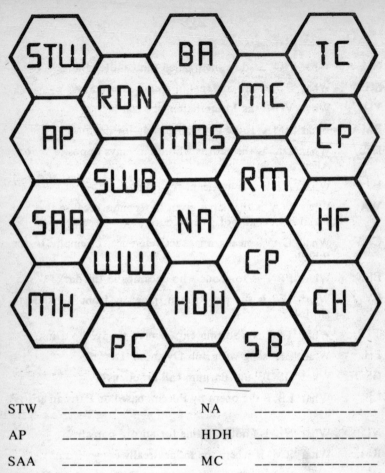

STW	_____	NA	_____
AP	_____	HDH	_____
SAA	_____	MC	_____
MH	_____	RM	_____
RDN	_____	CP	_____
SWB	_____	SB	_____
WW	_____	TC	_____
PC	_____	CP	_____
BA	_____	HF	_____
MAS	_____	CH	_____

STW: What 'STW' was a campaign initiated by Greenpeace?

AP: What 'AP' wrote 'To err is human, to forgive divine' and built his grotto at Twickenham?

SAA: What 'SAA' summons witnesses before Select Committees of the House of Commons?

MH: What 'MH' should we do while the sun shines?

RDN: What 'RDN' starred in the Martin Scorsese film *Taxi Driver*?

SWB: What 'SWB' defended the mission station at Rorke's Drift in the Zulu War?

WW: What 'WW' was the English poet whose home was in the Lake District?

PC: What 'PC' is used as an accompaniment to Italian dishes?

BA: What 'BA' is the only monkey native to Europe?

MAS: What 'MAS' has Lord Seiff as its Chairman?

NA: What 'NA' said 'A giant leap for mankind'?

HDH: What 'HDH' is a TV programme set in a holiday camp?

MC: What 'MC' was signed by King John at Runneymede?

RM: What 'RM' has opened a printing plant at Wapping in East London?

CP: What 'CP' is a houseplant with large leaves which you cannot eat?

SB: What 'SB' is the right hand side front on board ship?

TC: What 'TC' was the founder of Habitat?

CP: What 'CP' are on the south Kent coast and had Sir Winston Churchill as their Warden?

HF: What 'HF' means gunpowder has not burnt the main charge; or more commonly to delay?

CH: What 'CH' does a Member of Parliament apply for when he voluntarily resigns his seat?

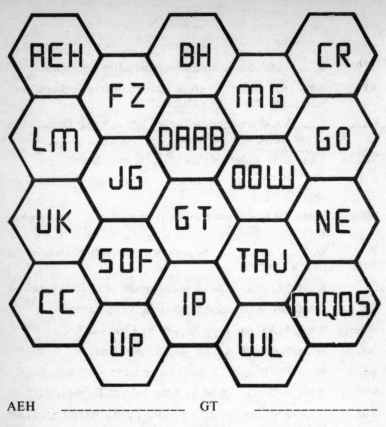

AEH	_____	GT	_____
LM	_____	IP	_____
UK	_____	MG	_____
CC	_____	OOW	_____
FZ	_____	TAJ	_____
JG	_____	WL	_____
SOF	_____	CR	_____
UP	_____	GO	_____
BH	_____	NE	_____
DAAB	_____	MQOS	_____

AEH: What 'AEH' wrote *A Shropshire Lad*?

LM: What 'LM' is a big Italian lake with Stresa on its shore?

UK: What 'UK' has the civil aircraft marking 'G'?

CC: What 'CC' have replaced the old Assizes?

FZ: What 'FZ' made the film *La Traviata* with Teresa Stratas?

JG: What 'JG' was a would-be President; ex-astronaut?

SOF: What 'SOF' is otherwise known as the Quakers?

UP: What 'UP' means a good golf score?

BH: What 'BH' sang with the Crickets?

DAAB: What 'DAAB' means mad as a hatter or nutty as a fruit cake?

GT: What 'GT' is a traveller who goes sightseeing all round the world?

IP: What 'IP' invented one sort of shorthand?

MG: What 'MG' was the author of *Cranford*?

OOW: What 'OOW' is where a fish can't swim?

TAJ: What 'TAJ' became better known as Simon and Garfunkel?

WL: What 'WL' is all the wavelengths of the spectrum combined?

CR: What 'CR' is the world's most famous bobsleigh track?

GO: What 'GO' wrote *Down and Out in Paris and London*?

NE: What 'NE' means money saved up?

MQOS: What 'MQOS' is the film in which Glenda and Vanessa are two monarchs?

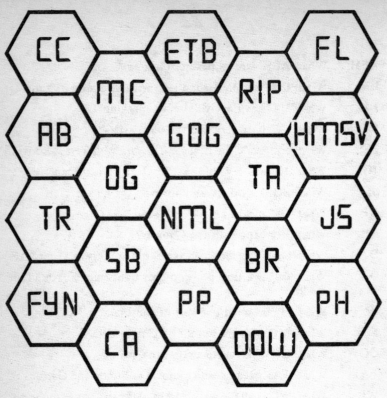

CC	_____	NML	_____
AB	_____	PP	_____
TR	_____	RIP	_____
FYN	_____	TA	_____
MC	_____	BR	_____
OG	_____	DOW	_____
SB	_____	FL	_____
CA	_____	HMSV	_____
ETB	_____	JS	_____
GOG	_____	PH	_____

CC: What 'CC' is a completely full football stadium?

AB: What 'AB' was an Austrian 19th century composer of huge symphonies?

TR: What 'TR' was the flower adopted as a badge by Henry VII?

FYN: What 'FYN' means to fill your house with luxuries as a result of nefarious activities?

MC: What 'MC' is the capital of Monaco?

OG: What 'OG' is the name used by some Americans for the US flag?

SB: What 'SB' is the Irish Nobel prize-winner whose characters waited for Godot?

CA: What 'CA' was the law of 1799 which sought to prevent the formation of Trades Unions?

ETB: What 'ETB' was said by Caesar when stabbed by his best mate?

GOG: What 'GOG' was the scene of Christ's agony on the Mount of Olives?

NML: What 'NML' means the area between two armies belonging to neither?

PP: What 'PP' is the book by Dickens that includes Mr Jingle, Mrs Bardell and Mr Snodgrass?

RIP: What 'RIP' means punishment in store, like onions in vinegar?

TA: What 'TA' is a person who never touches alcohol?

BR: What 'BR' is a plant metaphor for a person who is weak, and unreliable?

DOW: What 'DOW' was the Tory Prime Minister of George IV?

FL: What 'FL' is what the Americans call the President's wife?

HMSV: What 'HMSV' is Nelson's flag ship and still in commission?

JS: What 'JS' was Dean of St Patrick's, Dublin, who wrote *Gulliver's Travels*?

PH: What 'PH' made a 'Whiter Shade of Pale'?

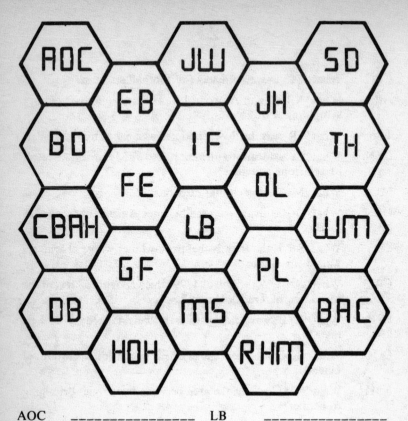

AOC	_____	LB	_____
BD	_____	MS	_____
CBAH	_____	JH	_____
DB	_____	OL	_____
EB	_____	PL	_____
FE	_____	RHM	_____
GF	_____	SD	_____
HOH	_____	TH	_____
JW	_____	WM	_____
IF	_____	BAC	_____

AOC: What 'AOC' was a Royal Wife nicknamed 'The Flemish or Flanders Mare'?

BD: What 'BD' is a Schottische performed in a farm building?

CBAH: What 'CBAH' tells you where Christian love starts?

DB: What 'DB' is a famous sand spit in the North Sea between Denmark and England?

EB: What 'EB' is the Ragtime composer and pianist who died in 1983?

FE: What 'FE' are throwing or jumping athletics not performed on a track?

GF: What 'GF' is a strong, lightweight and corrosion-resistant material used in boat and vehicle-body construction?

HOH: What 'HOH' is a much revered place, like the Caaba of Mecca?

JW: What 'JW' was a Sci-Fi writer who invented kids with yellow eyes and plants with a fatal sting?

IF: What 'IF' was the source of speculation in conjunction with an immovable object?

LB: What 'LB' was a golden boxing trophy donated by a Lord?

MS: What 'MS' was not Beethoven's name for his Opus No. 27 No. 2 for piano?

JH: What 'JH' was the first Englishman to trade in slaves?

OL: What 'OL' relates the flow of electric current to voltage?

PL: What 'PL' is Milton's most famous long poem?

RHM: What 'RHM' is indispensable male help and support?

SD: What 'SD' is the US equivalent of the Foreign Office?

TH: What 'TH' is responsible for English Lighthouses and Lightships?

WM: What 'WM' describes whiskers hanging down like those of a marine mammal?

BAC: What 'BAC' means two people taking it in turns to do something?

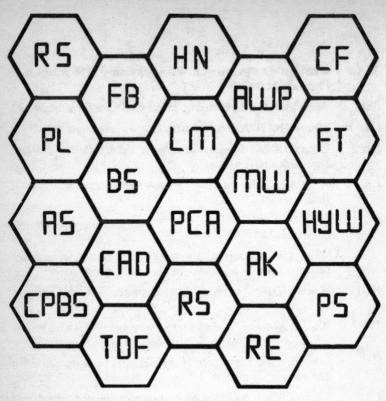

RS	————————————	PCA	————————————
PL	————————————	RS	————————————
AS	————————————	AWP	————————————
CPBS	————————————	MW	————————————
FB	————————————	AK	————————————
BS	————————————	RE	————————————
CAD	————————————	CF	————————————
TDF	————————————	FT	————————————
HN	————————————	HYW	————————————
LM	————————————	PS	————————————

RS: What 'RS' describes the phenomenon observed as light moves away from earth?

PL: What 'PL', author of *The Whitsun Weddings*, died in 1985?

AS: What 'AS' played the landlord in *The Young Ones*?

CPBS: What 'CPBS' means to waste one's words on the ignorant?

FB: What 'FB' were pilotless aircraft used in World War 2?

BS: What 'BS' was 'Born in the USA' in 1985?

CAD: What 'CAD' fall to earth during heavy storms?

TDF: What 'TDF' means literally the land of fire?

HN: What 'HN' is a wrestler's grip?

LM: What 'LM' played Sally Bowles in *Cabaret*?

PCA: What 'PCA' deals with complaints about government?

RS: What 'RS' at night is a shepherd's delight?

AWP: What 'AWP' features Geordies working on a building site in Germany?

MW: What 'MW' is made from grain and Highland spring water?

AK: What 'AK' was the founder of vast armaments factories at Essen?

RE: What 'RE' has as its motto the word Ubique, meaning, everywhere?

CF: What 'CF' is the black and white signal that a motor race is finished?

FT: What 'FT' is a chart of ancestors in arboreal form?

HYW: What 'HYW' started in 1337 and ended in 1453?

PS: What 'PS' means exerting an influence behind the scenes?

LLBS	_____	KKK	_____
GW	_____	SIT	_____
JOAT	_____	LQ	_____
LE	_____	JR	_____
PTQ	_____	FHTM	_____
SS	_____	AHAL	_____
WD	_____	TOTD	_____
OTBT	_____	PC	_____
JK	_____	JW	_____
LOH	_____	OFT	_____

LLBS: What 'LLBS' starring Noel Edmonds, is not seen at breakfast time on Saturdays?

GW: What 'GW' is fighting by small independently acting groups?

JOAT: What 'JOAT' can turn his hand to anything?

LE: What 'LE' is the Western point of Cornwall?

PTQ: What 'PTQ' means to propose marriage?

SS: What 'SS' is the faculty giving intuitive or extra-sensory knowledge?

WD: What 'WD' is a book by Richard Adams about a colony of rabbits?

OTBT: What 'OTBT' means miles away from anywhere?

JK: What 'JK', a member of the Beat Generation, wrote *On the Road*?

LOH: What 'LOH' is a ceremonial circuit of a football pitch by the winners?

KKK: What 'KKK' is the society hostile to negroes, originally formed in the Southern States of America, after the Civil War.

SIT: What 'SIT' saves nine?

LQ: What 'LQ' is the educational and artistic centre of Paris?

JR: What 'JR' is the pirates' black flag?

FHTM: What 'FHTM' means to live improvidently?

AHAL: What 'AHAL' means very cheerful?

TOTD: What 'TOTD' was a novel by Thomas Hardy and more recently a film starring Nastassia Kinski?

PC: What 'PC' was drummer with Genesis and now has a successful solo career?

JW: What 'JW' is a religious sect rejecting supremacy of state over religious principles?

OFT: What 'OFT' rises in Oxfordshire and departs at Gravesend?

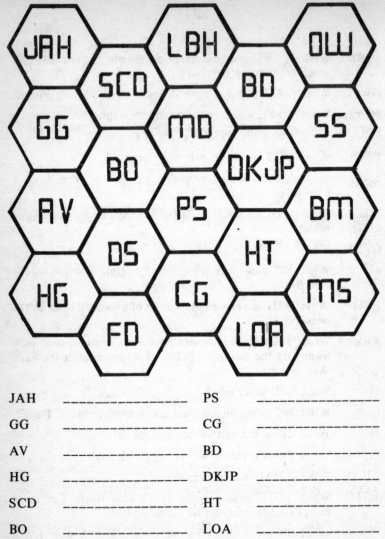

JAH	_____	PS	_____
GG	_____	CG	_____
AV	_____	BD	_____
HG	_____	DKJP	_____
SCD	_____	HT	_____
BO	_____	LOA	_____
DS	_____	OW	_____
FD	_____	SS	_____
LBH	_____	BM	_____
MD	_____	MS	_____

27

JAH: What 'JAH' means a single person in whom two personalities alternate?

GG: What 'GG' starred Richard Dreyfus and Marsha Mason, as reluctant flatsharers?

AV: What 'AV' is the Bible in English produced in 1611?

HG: What 'HG' is the third person of the Trinity – often represented as a dove?

SCD: What 'SCD' is the day on which Agincourt was fought?

BO: What 'BO' goes with Tim Brooke Taylor and Graeme Garden, on *The Goodies*?

DS: What 'DS' is the study of household management?

FD: What 'FD' is to signal to a vehicle to stop?

LBH: What 'LBH' means to memorise?

MD: What 'MD' is Herman Melville's classic about the search for a white whale?

PS: What 'PS' is seven days before Easter, when Christ entered Jerusalem?

CG: What 'CG' has a chemical element and a pungent smell?

BD: What 'BD' is the better known name of Robert Zimmerman – a singer?

DKJP: What 'DKJP' means are you acquainted with the most famous Cumberland huntsman?

HT: What 'HT' is the interval between two parts of a game?

LOA: What 'LOA' is the cartoon character created by Harold Gray who has a dog called Sandy?

OW: What 'OW' wrote the play containing the mythical Bunbury?

SS: What 'SS' is the popular name for the Espionage and Intelligence organisation?

BM: What 'BM' is the name of a Fascist dictator who was known as Il Duce?

MS: What 'MS' wrote *The Prime of Miss Jean Brodie*?

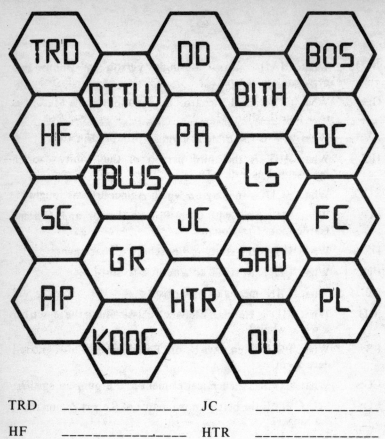

TRD	_____	JC	_____
HF	_____	HTR	_____
SC	_____	BITH	_____
AP	_____	LS	_____
DTTW	_____	SAD	_____
TBWS	_____	OU	_____
GR	_____	BOS	_____
KOOC	_____	DC	_____
DD	_____	FC	_____
PA	_____	PL	_____

28

TRD: What 'TRD' applies to animal fat boiled to clarify it?

HF: What 'HF' is a thanksgiving service for completion of the harvest?

SC: What 'SC' is a Parliamentary Committee with members from all parties?

AP: What 'AP' starred in *The Godfather* and *Dog Day Afternoon*?

DTTW: What 'DTTW' means unconscious or fast asleep?

TBWS: What 'TBWS' means to overawe by one's display of knowledge?

GR: What 'GR' was the dancing partner of Fred Astaire?

KOOC: What 'KOOC' means not to confide in others?

DD: What 'DD' sang the theme to the latest James Bond movie?

PA: What 'PA' means protection from arrest by another country?

JC: What 'JC' was President of the US before Ronald Reagan?

HTR: What 'HTR' means to become very angry?

BITH: What 'BITH' is better than two in the bush?

LS: What 'LS' is the largest or the best part?

SAD: What 'SAD' is the highwayman's command?

OU: What 'OU' is teaching mainly by broadcasting and correspondence, open to those without formal qualifications?

BOS: What 'BOS' was Figaro's occupation?

DC: What 'DC' is at an extremely low price?

FC: What 'FC' is the trophy of the 605 mile yacht race from the Isle of Wight to Plymouth?

PL: What 'PL' is versifier for Royal Household and State occasions?

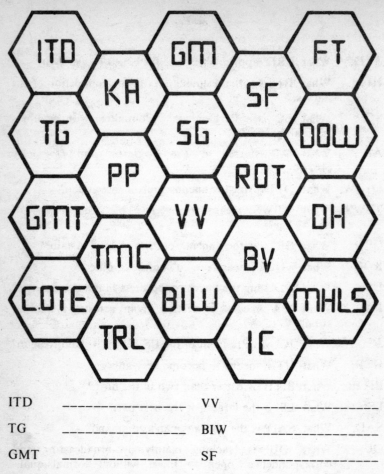

ITD	_____	VV	_____
TG	_____	BIW	_____
GMT	_____	SF	_____
COTE	_____	ROT	_____
KA	_____	BV	_____
PP	_____	IC	_____
TMC	_____	FT	_____
TRL	_____	DOW	_____
GM	_____	DH	_____
SG	_____	MHLS	_____

29

ITD: What 'ITD' means feeling blue or, alternatively, becalmed?

TG: What 'TG' means to show courage in adversity?

GMT: What 'GMT' is a system of standard time widely used instead of local time?

COTE: What 'COTE' is the Finance Minister in the British Government?

KA: What 'KA' wrote *Lucky Jim*?

PP: What 'PP' is a drama about the suffering and death of Christ?

TMC: What 'TMC' spoil the broth?

TRL: What 'TRL' was used to describe the British infantry during the Battle of Alma in the Crimean War?

GM: What 'GM', and subject of the Ken Russell film, wrote a symphony nicknamed 'Resurrection'?

SG: What 'SG' was defended by the Royal Marines during the Falklands War?

VV: What 'VV' means by oral examination?

BIW: What 'BIW' did the carrier in David Copperfield communicate to Peggotty?

SF: What 'SF' is the Irish Nationalist and Republican movement?

ROT: What 'ROT' means a rough but effective way of doing something?

BV: What 'BV' means have a pleasant journey?

IC: What 'IC' means in private?

FT: What 'FT' starred John Cleese and Prunella Scales as disaster-prone hotel proprietors?

DOW: What 'DOW' won the battle of Waterloo?

DH: What 'DH' is a race in which two or more winners finish exactly level?

MHLS: What 'MHLS' means that the best results are obtained by proceeding slowly and carefully?

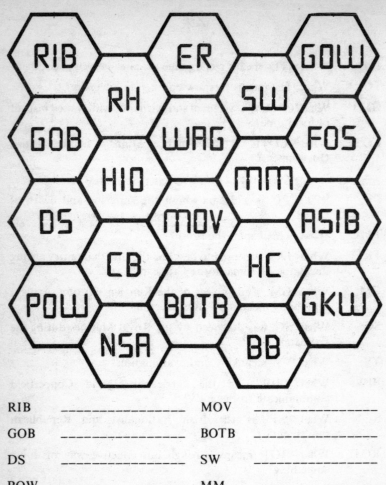

RIB	_____	MOV	_____
GOB	_____	BOTB	_____
DS	_____	SW	_____
POW	_____	MM	_____
RH	_____	HC	_____
HIO	_____	BB	_____
CB	_____	GOW	_____
NSA	_____	FOS	_____
ER	_____	ASIB	_____
WAG	_____	GKW	_____

30

RIB: What 'RIB' was a National Theatre play prosecuted for obscenity?

GOB: What 'GOB' means to outbid, or outdo someone?

DS: What 'DS' have had hits with 'Sultans of Swing' and 'Brothers in Arms'?

POW: What 'POW' is heir apparent to the British throne?

RH: What 'RH' is Deputy Leader of the Labour Party?

HIO: What 'HIO' means to get on well with someone?

CB: What 'CB' means negotiation of wages by an organised body of employees?

NSA: What 'NSA' means not subject to conditions?

ER: What 'ER' starring Michael Caine and Julie Walters was a film about the academic achievements of a working class girl?

WAG: What 'WAG' do learned counsel wear in court?

MOV: What 'MOV' by Shakespeare has Portia as the protagonist?

BOTB: What 'BOTB' prevented the German Army from counter-attacking during the Normandy Campaign in World War 2?

SW: What 'SW' was the subject of a play by Arthur Miller called *The Crucible*?

MM: What 'MM' is the unlikely female sleuth in Agatha Christie's detective stories?

HC: What 'HC' means the option of taking what is offered or nothing?

BB: What 'BB' is an Australian inlet off New South Wales at which James Cook landed?

GOW: What 'GOW' did the Lord tread upon in the vineyard where they were stored?

FOS: What 'FOS' are assembled ships and not a speedy cut price?

ASIB: What 'ASIB' was a successful remake of a 1930's movie starring Barbra Streisand and Kris Kristofferson?

GKW: What 'GKW' looked out on the feast of Stephen?

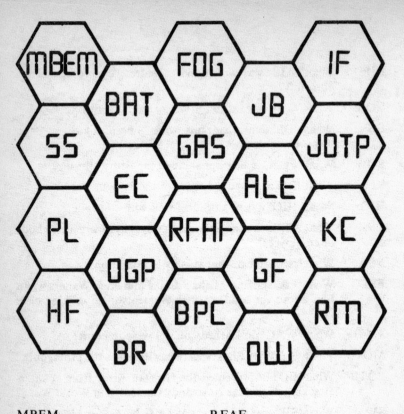

MBEM	_____	RFAF	_____
SS	_____	BPC	_____
PL	_____	JB	_____
HF	_____	ALE	_____
BAT	_____	GF	_____
EC	_____	OW	_____
OGP	_____	IF	_____
BR	_____	JOTP	_____
FOG	_____	KC	_____
GAS	_____	RM	_____

31

MBEM: What 'MBEM' means to live within one's income?

SS: What 'SS' is Rocky?

PL: What 'PL' is a body of men stationed by a trade union to dissuade men from working during a strike?

HF: What 'HF' means to speak at great length?

BAT: What 'BAT' was the armed force recruited to fight Sinn Fein in 1921?

EC: What 'EC' has a silver lining?

OGP: What 'OGP' was Henry Fonda's last film?

BR: What 'BR' is the Gentleman Usher of Lord Chamberlain's Department in the House of Lords?

FOG: What 'FOG' made a racket and saved Rome from invasion?

GAS: What 'GAS' wrote music and lyrics for the Savoy Operas?

RFAF: What 'RFAF' means to act recklessly?

BPC: What 'BPC' sailed over the sea to Skye?

JB: What 'JB' was the celebrated negro singer who starred with the Folies Bergère?

ALE: What 'ALE' means bored or without definite occupation?

GF: What 'GF' is Premier of Eire?

OW: What 'OW' starred in and directed *A Touch of Evil*?

IF: What 'IF' is an idea that dominates the mind?

JOTP: What 'JOTP' sits on the bench?

KC: What 'KC' means not to be flustered or to panic?

RM: What 'RM' is the corps trained for service at sea and on land?

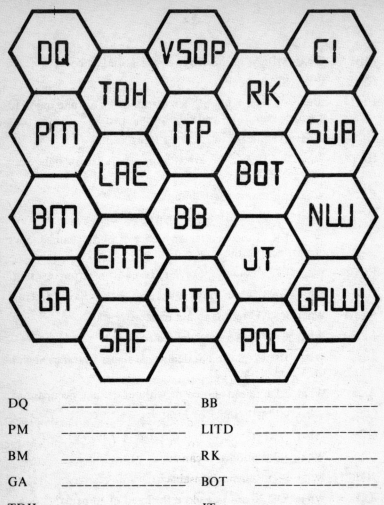

DQ	_____	BB	_____
PM	_____	LITD	_____
BM	_____	RK	_____
GA	_____	BOT	_____
TDH	_____	JT	_____
LAE	_____	POC	_____
EMF	_____	CI	_____
SAF	_____	SUA	_____
VSOP	_____	NW	_____
ITP	_____	GAWI	_____

32

DQ: What 'DQ' was a novel by Cervantes and a hit single by Nik Kershaw?

PM: What 'PM' is a dessert named after a famous Australian opera singer?

BM: What 'BM' is illegitimate traffic in officially controlled goods?

GA: What 'GA' is an indeterminate point of dispute?

TDH: What 'TDH' is a film about Vietnam, not about blood-sports?

LAE: What 'LAE' means to listen?

EMF: What 'EMF' wrote a novel about the Raj, recently an award-winning film?

SAF: What 'SAF' is an area of unstable rock threatening to engulf San Francisco?

VSOP: What 'VSOP' is a rare and expensive brandy?

ITP: What 'ITP' means fully informed?

BB: What 'BB' is an aircraft flight recorder?

LITD: What 'LITD' is a rash experiment?

RK: What 'RK' wrote *The Jungle Book*?

BOT: What 'BOT' lost England its most famous Admiral in 1805?

JT: What 'JT' was forced to resign from the leadership of the Liberal Party after a scandal?

POC: What 'POC' is indispensable for gamblers?

CI: What 'CI' means to yield to pressure or to submit?

SUA: What 'SUA' is Shakespeare's birthplace?

NW: What 'NW' is a self help group organised to prevent crime?

GAWI: What 'GAWI' means to escape retribution?

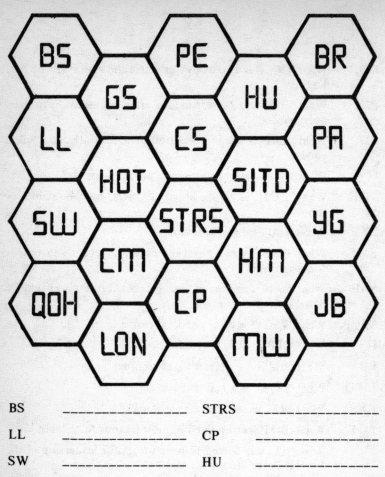

BS	_____	STRS	_____
LL	_____	CP	_____
SW	_____	HU	_____
QOH	_____	SITD	_____
GS	_____	HM	_____
HOT	_____	MW	_____
CM	_____	BR	_____
LON	_____	PA	_____
PE	_____	YG	_____
CS	_____	JB	_____

33

BS: What 'BS' is a scoundrel, or an unsatisfactory member of a family?

LL: What 'LL' wrote *Cider with Rosie*?

SW: What 'SW' was the film of the adventures of Luke Skywalker?

QOH: What 'QOH' terrorised Alice in *Alice in Wonderland*?

GS: What 'GS' are Grandma's apples?

HOT: What 'HOT' had the face that launched a thousand ships?

CM: What 'CM', a famous dramatist and poet, was killed in a pub brawl in Deptford?

LON: What 'LON' means to be in a deep sleep?

PE: What 'PE' plays Jim Hacker in *Yes, Prime Minister*?

CS: What 'CS' led an ill-fated expedition to the South Pole in 1909?

STRS: What 'STRS' means to correct a misapprehension?

CP: What 'CP' is a bird used for conveying messages?

HU: What 'HU' means poor, lacking money?

SITD: What 'SITD' is a mere guess?

HM: What 'HM' coined the phrase 'You've never had it so good'?

MW: What 'MW', the wife of a former Prime Minister, is a well-known poet?

BR: What 'BR' was filmed at Castle Howard, Yorkshire, in 1981?

PA: What 'PA' rode the show-jumper, Doublet?

YG: What 'YG' was the first man to orbit the earth?

JB: What 'JB' was the policewoman heroine created by Molly Hardwick?

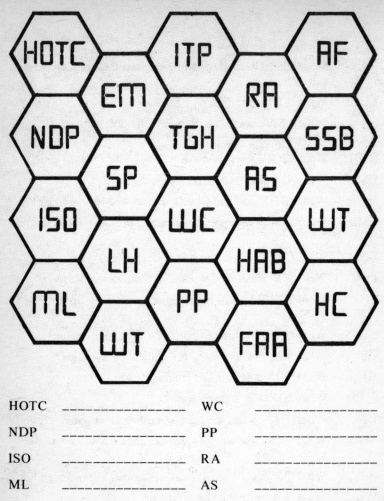

HOTC   ——————————   WC   ——————————

NDP   ——————————   PP   ——————————

ISO   ——————————   RA   ——————————

ML   ——————————   AS   ——————————

EM   ——————————   HAB   ——————————

SP   ——————————   FAA   ——————————

LH   ——————————   AF   ——————————

WT   ——————————   SSB   ——————————

ITP   ——————————   WT   ——————————

TGH   ——————————   HC   ——————————

34

HOTC: What 'HOTC' means to reprimand?

NDP: What 'NDP' is a writer's pseudonym?

ISO: What 'ISO' means notwithstanding?

ML: What 'ML' is the most looked-at painting in the Louvre?

EM: What 'EM' does Melina Mercouri want the British to give back?

SP: What 'SP' is England's highest mountain?

LH: What 'LH' plays JR in 'Dallas'?

WT: What 'WT' was the subject of a Rossini opera?

ITP: What 'ITP' means in very good health?

TGH: What 'TGH' is a cowboy's headgear?

WC: What 'WC' was the first British Prime Minister to serve under Queen Elizabeth II?

PP: What 'PP' was the hero of a play by J.M. Barrie?

RA: What 'RA' is a European species of butterfly?

AS: What 'AS' succeeded Nasser as President of Egypt?

HAB: What 'HAB' means agitated and exasperated?

FAA: What 'FAA' immortalised the song 'Underneath the Arches'?

AF: What 'AF' discovered Penicillin?

SSB: What 'SSB', floated in the eighteenth century, burst and ruined thousands?

WT: What 'WT' led the Peasants' Revolt in 1381?

HC: What 'HC' is traditionally associated with a schoolboy sport played with its fruit?

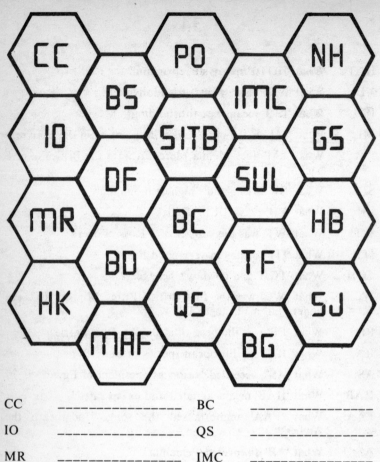

CC _____   BC _____

IO _____   QS _____

MR _____   IMC _____

HK _____   SUL _____

BS _____   TF _____

DF _____   BG _____

BD _____   NH _____

MAF _____   GS _____

PO _____   HB _____

SITB _____   SJ _____

35

CC: What 'CC' have they still not found the cure for?

IO: What 'IO' is a sea contested by the great Powers' navies?

MR: What 'MR' ended in the battle of Sedgemoor and the execution of its hero, the illegitimate son of Charles II?

HK: What 'HK' was the former US Secretary of State who wrote a book of memoirs entitled *The White House Years*?

BS: What 'BS' are Belgian brassica?

DF: What 'DF' is an imitation insect for catching trout?

BD: What 'BD' became the youngest woman ever elected to the British Parliament in 1969?

MAF: What 'MAF' means to grimace?

PO: What 'PO' is the naval equivalent of an Army sergeant?

SITB: What 'SITB' is an unexpected wounding from behind with a knife?

BC: What 'BC' overcame cancer and won the 1981 Grand National?

QS: What 'QS' estimates the amounts of material used in building?

IMC: What 'IMC' means fresh, unsoiled or perfect?

SUL: What 'SUL' means firmness or fortitude?

TF: What 'TF' means solid ground?

BG: What 'BG' organised Live Aid?

NH: What 'NH' is the study of animals and plants?

GS: What 'GS' is a kind and helpful person?

HB: What 'HB' starred as the university drop-out in *Shelley*?

SJ: What 'SJ' composed the theme music used for *The Sting*?

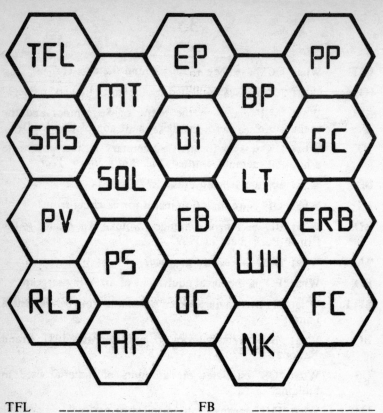

TFL	_____	FB	_____
SAS	_____	OC	_____
PV	_____	BP	_____
RLS	_____	LT	_____
MT	_____	WH	_____
SOL	_____	NK	_____
PS	_____	PP	_____
FAF	_____	GC	_____
EP	_____	ERB	_____
DI	_____	FC	_____

36

TFL: What 'TFL' means to depart or act without having permission or giving notice?

SAS: What 'SAS' means unharmed or uninjured?

PV: What 'PV' means a success that turns out to have been a failure?

RLS: What 'RLS' wrote *Dr Jekyll and Mr Hyde*?

MT: What 'MT' is the famous museum in London's Baker Street?

SOL: What 'SOL' means at some time or other?

PS: What 'PS' wrote *Prometheus Unbound* and drowned off the Italian coast in 1822?

FAF: What 'FAF' means to make friends with someone after a quarrel?

EP: What 'EP' was the South American political figure on whom a musical was based?

DI: What 'DI' was the notorious French penal settlement where Dreyfus was sent?

FB: What 'FB' is a nuclear reactor that manufactures its own plutonium fuel?

OC: What 'OC' was the name of the massive police investigation into police corruption?

BP: What 'BP' created Peter Rabbit?

LT: What 'LT' is another meaning for currency?

WH: What 'WH', the novel, contains the character Heathcliffe?

NK: What 'NK' was Australia's most infamous bush ranger?

PP: What 'PP' stars Peter Sellers as an incompetent French detective?

GC: What 'GC' is the military honour for bravery?

ERB: What 'ERB' was the author who created Tarzan?

FC: What 'FC' is killed for a returning prodigal?

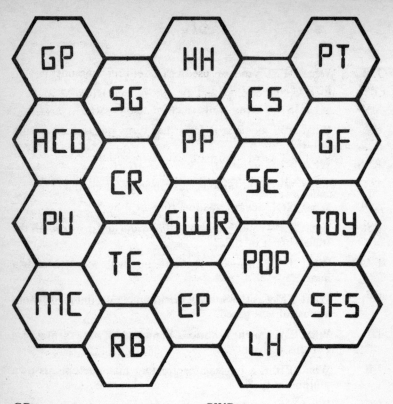

GP	_____	SWR	_____
ACD	_____	EP	_____
PU	_____	CS	_____
MC	_____	SE	_____
SG	_____	POP	_____
CR	_____	LH	_____
TE	_____	PT	_____
RB	_____	GF	_____
HH	_____	TOY	_____
PP	_____	SFS	_____

37

GP: What 'GP' is a person used in a scientific experiment?

ACD: What 'ACD' was the creator of Sherlock Holmes?

PU: What 'PU' is a brawl?

MC: What 'MC' is an international system of signalling?

SG: What 'SG' is an informant with a lot to impart?

CR: What 'CR' was the founder of the country now known as Zimbabwe?

TE: What 'TE' was hanged in 1950 and pardoned in 1966?

RB: What 'RB' wrote *Home Thoughts From Abroad*?

HH: What 'HH' headed the Gestapo?

PP: What 'PP' was a celebrated Cubist painter?

SWR: What 'SWR', a 17th century explorer, introduced tobacco into this country?

EP: What 'EP' is where the used gases escape from a car engine?

CS: What 'CS' is a series of twelve consecutive semitones?

SE: What 'SE' is the instruction given to squaddies, telling them to relax?

POP: What 'POP' is made of gypsum and used for moulds and casts?

LH: What 'LH' was the first pro to captain England at cricket?

PT: What 'PT' is TV's best known gardener?

GF: What 'GF' comes at the end of a pantomime or variety show?

TOY: What 'TOY' was Vera Brittain's serialised autobiography?

SFS: What 'SFS' means to begin at the beginning?

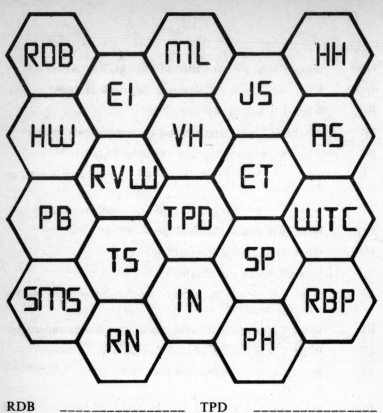

RDB	_____	TPD	_____
HW	_____	IN	_____
PB	_____	JS	_____
SMS	_____	ET	_____
EI	_____	SP	_____
RVW	_____	PH	_____
TS	_____	HH	_____
RN	_____	AS	_____
ML	_____	WTC	_____
VH	_____	RBP	_____

38

RDB: What 'RDB' was a barrister who wrote *Lorna Doone*?

HW: What 'HW' is the everyday name for deuterium oxide?

PB: What 'PB' is the old-fashioned name for a bicycle?

SMS: What 'SMS' was the adored Prom conductor known as 'Flash'?

EI: What 'EI' is the poetic name for Ireland?

RVW: What 'RVW' nodded off in the mountains for twenty years?

TS: What 'TS' lies between New Zealand and Australia?

RN: What 'RN' played the title role in Ken Russell's *Valentino*?

ML: What 'ML' was the German leader of the Protestant Reformation?

VH: What 'VH' wrote *The Hunchback of Notre Dame*?

TPD: What 'TPD' was Britain's first National Park?

IN: What 'IN' was inspired to delve into gravity after being hit on the head by an apple?

JS: What 'JS' won a Pulitzer Prize for his novel *The Grapes of Wrath*?

ET: What 'ET' is a famous Parisian landmark?

SP: What 'SP' is where Stonehenge is situated?

PH: What 'PH' was attacked by Admiral Yamamoto?

HH: What 'HH' is found on Lonely Street?

AS: What 'AS' was the Russian writer deported from the Soviet Union in 1974?

WTC: What 'WTC' was England's first Norman King?

RBP: What 'RBP' was the founder of the Scout movement?

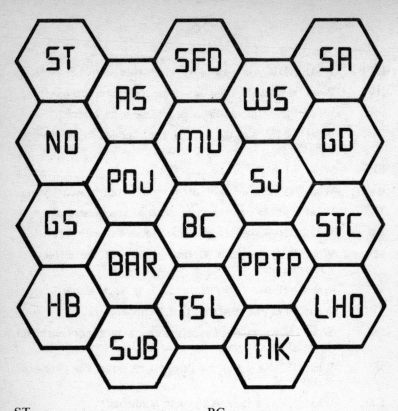

ST	_____	BC	_____
NO	_____	TSL	_____
GS	_____	WS	_____
HB	_____	SJ	_____
AS	_____	PPTP	_____
POJ	_____	MK	_____
BAR	_____	SA	_____
SJB	_____	GD	_____
SFD	_____	STC	_____
MU	_____	LHO	_____

39

ST: What 'ST' helps Scotland Yard on *Police Five*?

NO: What 'NO' is the city which lies at the mouth of the Mississippi River?

GS: What 'GS' created the *Maigret* detective stories?

HB: What 'HB' is the only bird that can fly backwards?

AS: What 'AS' is the translation of après soleil?

POJ: What 'POJ' means long suffering tolerance?

BAR: What 'BAR' means to abandon an undertaking?

SJB: What 'SJB' succeeded Cecil Day Lewis as Poet Laureate?

SFD: What 'SFD' circled the world in the Golden Hind?

MU: What 'MU' were the first English soccer club to win the European cup?

BC: What 'BC' is the Westernmost province of Canada?

TSL: What 'TSL' is another name for the Aurora Australis?

WS: What 'WS' is Britain's largest prison?

SJ: What 'SJ' said 'When a man is tired of London, he is tired of life!'?

PPTP: What 'PPTP' means to begin writing?

MK: What 'MK' is the highest mountain in Africa?

SA: What 'SA' is the period when all implements were made of minerals?

GD: What 'GD' is trained to bring in game?

STC: What 'STC' means to refuse to associate with a person?

LHO: What 'LHO' is supposed to have killed President Kennedy?

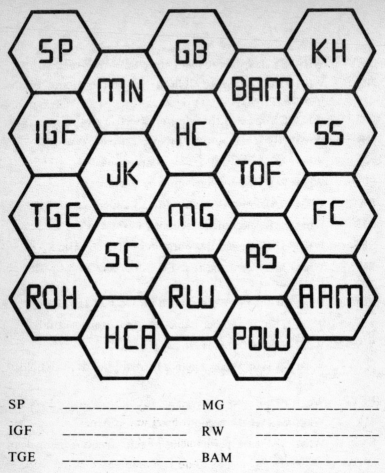

SP	_____	MG	_____
IGF	_____	RW	_____
TGE	_____	BAM	_____
ROH	_____	TOF	_____
MN	_____	AS	_____
JK	_____	POW	_____
SC	_____	KH	_____
HCA	_____	SS	_____
GB	_____	FC	_____
HC	_____	AAM	_____

40

SP: What 'SP' is a red flower as well as a book?

IGF: What 'IGF' means in all honesty?

TGE: What 'TGE' was a film set in a prison camp, starring Steve McQueen?

ROH: What 'ROH' commemorates the dead of two world wars?

MN: What 'MN' does a compass needle point to?

JK: What 'JK' was the mediaeval hangman?

SC: What 'SC' is the patron saint of travellers?

HCA: What 'HCA' wrote *The Ugly Duckling*?

GB: What 'GB' was the Argentine ship sunk during the Falklands War?

HC: What 'HC' was last seen in 1985?

MG: What 'MG' was invented during the late 19th century for rapid firing?

RW: What 'RW' was the Greenpeace ship blown up in New Zealand?

BAM: What 'BAM' were the two spies who escaped to Moscow in 1956?

TOF: What 'TOF' is the Frederick Forsyth novel about a German journalist searching for a Nazi war criminal?

AS: What 'AS' played Manuel in *Fawlty Towers*?

POW: What 'POW' means to do one's fair share of the work?

KH: What 'KH' was the place the Wright brothers flew from?

SS: What 'SS' means the time when newspapers are short of news?

FC: What 'FC' is the Premier of Cuba?

AAM: What 'AAM' wrote *Winnie the Pooh*?

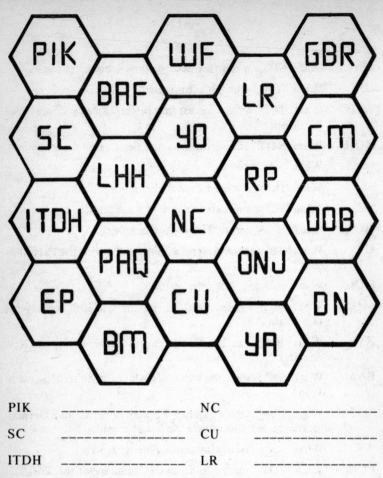

PIK	‾‾‾‾‾‾‾‾‾‾‾‾‾‾	NC	‾‾‾‾‾‾‾‾‾‾‾‾‾‾
SC	‾‾‾‾‾‾‾‾‾‾‾‾‾‾	CU	‾‾‾‾‾‾‾‾‾‾‾‾‾‾
ITDH	‾‾‾‾‾‾‾‾‾‾‾‾‾‾	LR	‾‾‾‾‾‾‾‾‾‾‾‾‾‾
EP	‾‾‾‾‾‾‾‾‾‾‾‾‾‾	RP	‾‾‾‾‾‾‾‾‾‾‾‾‾‾
BAF	‾‾‾‾‾‾‾‾‾‾‾‾‾‾	ONJ	‾‾‾‾‾‾‾‾‾‾‾‾‾‾
LHH	‾‾‾‾‾‾‾‾‾‾‾‾‾‾	YA	‾‾‾‾‾‾‾‾‾‾‾‾‾‾
PAQ	‾‾‾‾‾‾‾‾‾‾‾‾‾‾	GBR	‾‾‾‾‾‾‾‾‾‾‾‾‾‾
BM	‾‾‾‾‾‾‾‾‾‾‾‾‾‾	CM	‾‾‾‾‾‾‾‾‾‾‾‾‾‾
WF	‾‾‾‾‾‾‾‾‾‾‾‾‾‾	OOB	‾‾‾‾‾‾‾‾‾‾‾‾‾‾
YO	‾‾‾‾‾‾‾‾‾‾‾‾‾‾	DN	‾‾‾‾‾‾‾‾‾‾‾‾‾‾

41

PIK: What 'PIK' means rewarded by goods rather than money?

SC: What 'SC' was the waterway closed by Nasser in 1956?

ITDH: What 'ITDH' means in disgrace?

EP: What 'EP' is the official residence of the President of France?

BAF: What 'BAF' means to lose one's temper?

LHH: What 'LHH' broadcasted German propaganda during World War 2?

PAQ: What 'PAQ' means to find a pretext for an argument?

BM: What 'BM' are a German terrorist group?

WF: What 'WF' was a famous US pioneer stagecoach line?

YO: What 'YO' was married to John Lennon?

NC: What 'NC' brought the message 'Peace in our time'?

CU: What 'CU' means to summon to serve in the Army?

LR: What 'LR' portrayed Reggie Perrin and Rigsby?

RP: What 'RP' houses London's Zoo?

ONJ: What 'ONJ' starred with John Travolta in *Grease*?

YA: What 'YA' is the leader of the PLO?

GBR: What 'GBR' is the world's largest coral reef?

CM: What 'CM' means made to measure?

OOB: What 'OOB' means beyond the permitted area?

DN: What 'DN' is the more common name for the plant belladonna?

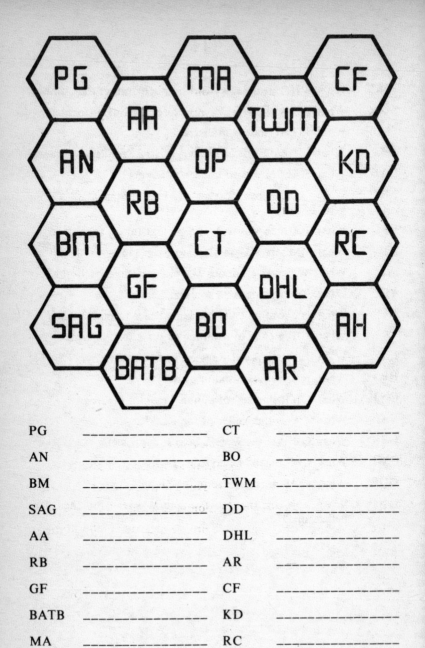

PG   ——————————   CT   ——————————

AN   ——————————   BO   ——————————

BM   ——————————   TWM   ——————————

SAG   ——————————   DD   ——————————

AA   ——————————   DHL   ——————————

RB   ——————————   AR   ——————————

GF   ——————————   CF   ——————————

BATB   ——————————   KD   ——————————

MA   ——————————   RC   ——————————

OP   ——————————   AH   ——————————

42

PG: What 'PG' climbed up on Salisbury Hill?

AN: What 'AN' invented dynamite and inaugurated a famous prize?

BM: What 'BM' defeated Rommel at El Alamein?

SAG: What 'SAG' sang 'Scarborough Fair'?

AA: What 'AA' is a comedy about the French Resistance?

RB: What 'RB' played a convict in *Porridge*?

GF: What 'GF' is a general office clerk?

BATB: What 'BATB' means to approach a subject slowly or to prevaricate?

MA: What 'MA' said 'Let them eat cake!'?

OP: What 'OP' was the film starring and directed by Robert Redford?

CT: What 'CT' is the thick black liquid made from coal?

BO: What 'BO' is a monastic group, and also makes a sweet liqueur?

TWM: What 'TWM' followed the star?

DD: What 'DD' is where ships undergo a refit?

DHL: What 'DHL' wrote *Sons and Lovers*?

AR: What 'AR' is the means of approach to a place?

CF: What 'CF' has a waxy skin and acidic juice?

KD: What 'KD' is a percussion instrument?

RC: What 'RC' created the private detective Philip Marlowe?

AH: What 'AH' is named after Queen Victoria's consort?

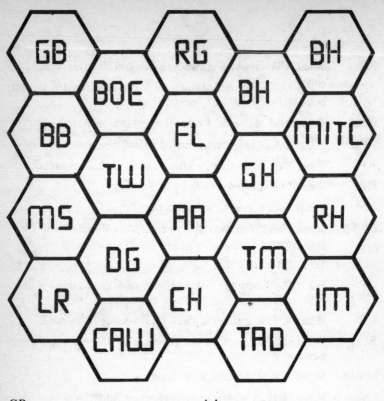

GB	_____	AA	_____
BB	_____	CH	_____
MS	_____	BH	_____
LR	_____	GH	_____
BOE	_____	TM	_____
TW	_____	TAD	_____
DG	_____	BH	_____
CAW	_____	MITC	_____
RG	_____	RH	_____
FL	_____	IM	_____

43

GB: What 'GB' was the nickname for US Special Forces in Vietnam?

BB: What 'BB' is London's most famous clock?

MS: What 'MS' is Britain's Communist daily newspaper?

LR: What 'LR' is the annual list of ships of various classes?

BOE: What 'BOE' is called the Old Lady of Threadneedle Street?

TW: What 'TW' is the Archbishop of Canterbury's special envoy?

DG: What 'DG' keeps out the noise and the cold?

CAW: What 'CAW' were eaten by Little Miss Muffett?

RG: What 'RG' wrote *I Claudius*?

FL: What 'FL' should drivers move into to arrive early?

AA: What 'AA' is water?

CH: What 'CH' is used to combine reaping and threshing?

BH: What 'BH' is the British Grand Prix racing course?

GH: What 'GH' do you not look in the mouth?

TM: What 'TM' was Britain's longest running play?

TAD: What 'TAD' were the ice dancing duo who won the European and World titles in 1981 and 1982?

BH: What 'BH' is believed to have been created when a star collapses?

MITC: What 'MITC' is the T.S. Eliot play set in Canterbury Cathedral?

RH: What 'RH' was Spandau Prison's last inmate?

IM: What 'IM' is a rock group, and was also a mediaeval form of torture?

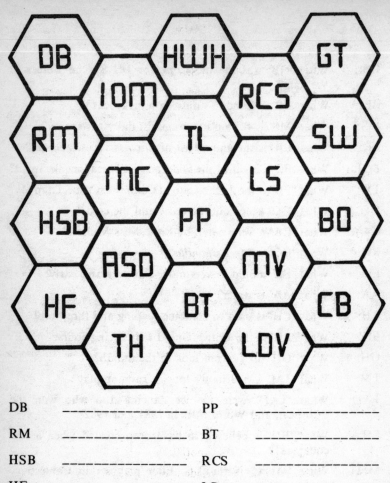

DB	------------------	PP	------------------
RM	------------------	BT	------------------
HSB	------------------	RCS	------------------
HF	------------------	LS	------------------
IOM	------------------	MV	------------------
MC	------------------	LDV	------------------
ASD	------------------	GT	------------------
TH	------------------	SW	------------------
HWH	------------------	BO	------------------
TL	------------------	CB	------------------

44

DB: What 'DB' is a North Sea fishing ground?

RM: What 'RM' is where steel bar is turned into sheet?

HSB: What 'HSB' is a long-running TV series about American cops?

HF: What 'HF' starred in the film *Raiders of the Lost Ark*?

IOM: What 'IOM' is where the tail-less cats come from?

MC: What 'MC' crashed his boat *Bluebird* on Lake Coniston?

ASD: What 'ASD' is the 1st of November?

TH: What 'TH' is the current Poet Laureate?

HWH: What 'HWH' is an inn midway between towns, or a possible compromise?

TL: What 'TL' is lit at Hallowe'en?

PP: What 'PP' is the Treasury?

BT: What 'BT' is the reputedly haunted area of sea off Florida?

RCS: What 'RCS' do you see through if you take a cheerful view of life?

LS: What 'LS' is soonest mended?

MV: What 'MV' erupted to destroy Pompeii?

LDV: What 'LDV' painted the Mona Lisa?

GT: What 'GT' deserves another?

SW: What 'SW' is the President of the SDP?

BO: What 'BO' is a kind of biscuit?

CB: What 'CB' means authorisation to do what you want?

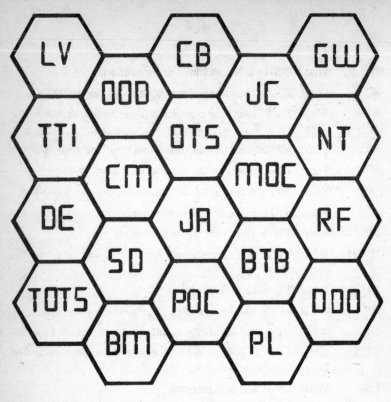

LV	_____	JA	_____
TTI	_____	POC	_____
DE	_____	JC	_____
TOTS	_____	MOC	_____
OOD	_____	BTB	_____
CM	_____	PL	_____
SD	_____	GW	_____
BM	_____	NT	_____
CB	_____	RF	_____
OTS	_____	DOO	_____

45

LV: What 'LV' is the largest lake in Africa?

TTI: What 'TTI' is the disaster movie starring Steve McQueen and Paul Newman?

DE: What 'DE' is a phrase capable of two meanings?

TOTS: What 'TOTS' is a famous short novel by Henry James?

OOD: What 'OOD' means in the open air?

CM: What 'CM' is a period of time within a year?

SD: What 'SD' is the famous snooker player?

BM: What 'BM' is where the Magna Carta is kept?

CB: What 'CB' is an avian in captivity?

OTS: What 'OTS' is the phrase used of someone not yet married and over a certain age?

JA: What 'JA' is the actress playing the title role in *Mary Poppins*?

POC: What 'POC' is something easily managed?

JC: What 'JC' was *A Boy Named Sue*?

MOC: What 'MOC' is a character of quality?

BTB: What 'BTB' means to demand an explanation?

PL: What 'PL' is the 'official version'?

GW: What 'GW' started with the assassination of an Archduke?

NT: What 'NT' brought the Nazis to justice?

RF: What 'RF' are the stormy part of the Atlantic, also a film?

DOO: What 'DOO' is a disagreement?

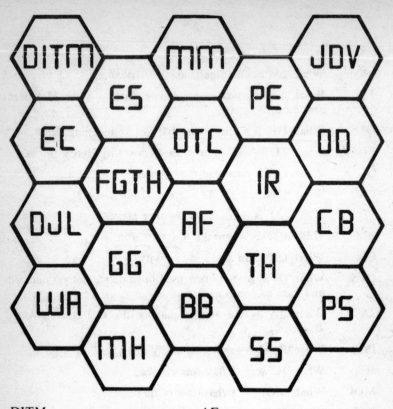

DITM	_____	AF	_____
EC	_____	BB	_____
DJL	_____	PE	_____
WA	_____	IR	_____
ES	_____	TH	_____
FGTH	_____	SS	_____
GG	_____	JDV	_____
MH	_____	OD	_____
MM	_____	CB	_____
OTC	_____	PS	_____

46

DITM: What 'DITM' means out of spirits?

EC: What 'EC' played with Cream and is now a solo performer?

DJL: What 'DJL' is on the sea bed?

WA: What 'WA' is where Queen Elizabeth II was crowned?

ES: What 'ES' is the planet Venus?

FGTH: What 'FGTH' had a hit with 'The Power of Love'?

GG: What 'GG' wrote *Brighton Rock*?

MH: What 'MH' are you as mad as?

MM: What 'MM' does Mel Gibson star in?

OTC: What 'OTC' means without preparation?

AF: What 'AF' is the historian married to Harold Pinter?

BB: What 'BB' was the 'Fat Owl' of Greyfriars?

PE: What 'PE' are one's own property?

IR: What 'IR' were the economic changes of the 18th century?

TH: What 'TH' was famous for his *Blood Donor* sketch?

SS: What 'SS' is the legendary song of a dying royal bird?

JDV: What 'JDV' means enjoyment of life?

OD: What 'OD' is a festive occasion when a school admits visitors?

CB: What 'CB' is a potato pest?

PS: What 'PS' is the comedienne married to Billy Connolly?

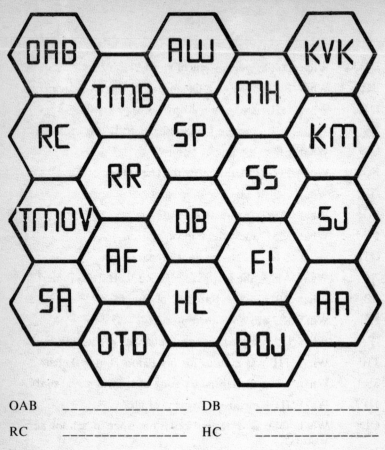

OAB	_____	DB	_____
RC	_____	HC	_____
TMOV	_____	MH	_____
SA	_____	SS	_____
TMB	_____	FI	_____
RR	_____	BOJ	_____
AF	_____	KVK	_____
OTD	_____	KM	_____
AW	_____	SJ	_____
SP	_____	AA	_____

47

OAB: What 'OAB' is a slot machine for gambling?

RC: What 'RC' works machinery at a distance?

TMOV: What 'TMOV' contains 'the quality of mercy'?

SA: What 'SA' are weapons carried by one man?

TMB: What 'TMB' starred in *Duck Soup*?

RR: What 'RR' has as its hero Alan Breck?

AF: What 'AF' is an illness originating in China?

OTD: What 'OTD' means punctually?

AW: What 'AW' is a famous poem by T.S. Eliot and is the day after Shrove Tuesday?

SP: What 'SP' was a 17th century diarist?

DB: What 'DB' starred in *Merry Christmas Mr Lawrence*?

HC: What 'HC' discovered the tomb of Tutankhamun?

MH: What 'MH' gets you less speed?

SS: What 'SS' won the Eurovision Song Contest with 'Puppet on a String'?

FI: What 'FI' are the chain of islands off the Dutch Coast?

BOJ: What 'BOJ' was where the Navy met the Grand Fleet in World War I?

KVK: What 'KVK' was the film starring Meryl Streep and Dustin Hoffman?

KM: What 'KM' wrote *Das Kapital*?

SJ: What 'SJ' was the nickname for the first spinning machine?

AA: What 'AA' is a breed of Scottish cattle?

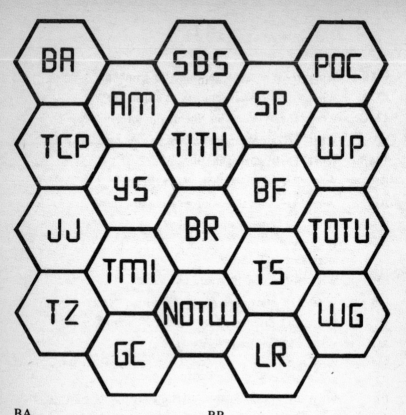

BA	_____		BR	_____
TCP	_____		NOTW	_____
JJ	_____		SP	_____
TZ	_____		BF	_____
AM	_____		TS	_____
YS	_____		LR	_____
TMI	_____		POC	_____
GC	_____		WP	_____
SBS	_____		TOTU	_____
TITH	_____		WG	_____

48

BA: What 'BA' is a snake, and also a TV programme starring Rowan Atkinson?

TCP: What 'TCP' are careers such as nursing and social work?

JJ: What 'JJ' is a large passenger-carrying aircraft?

TZ: What 'TZ' are astrological signs?

AM: What 'AM' was the composer who was the subject of a play by Peter Shaffer?

YS: What 'YS' was a Beatles' film and song?

TMI: What 'TMI' was the site of a major nuclear accident in the USA?

GC: What 'GC' is one's ancestor's timepiece?

SBS: What 'SBS' is the navy's crack force?

TITH: What 'TITH' is a dish made with sausages and batter?

BR: What 'BR' is a Northumbrian folk song?

NOTW: What 'NOTW' is a popular Sunday newspaper?

SP: What 'SP' is a houseplant, not an insect?

BF: What 'BF' is a solo artist, who was once with Roxy Music?

TS: What 'TS' is an exaggerated tale?

LR: What 'LR' had an Indian companion called Tonto?

POC: What 'POC' is a metal instrument used for measuring and drawing, usually circles?

WP: What 'WP' is a bird which is found in woodlands which can be eaten?

TOTU: What 'TOTU' is a series of horror stories by Roald Dahl?

WG: What 'WG' means day-dreaming?

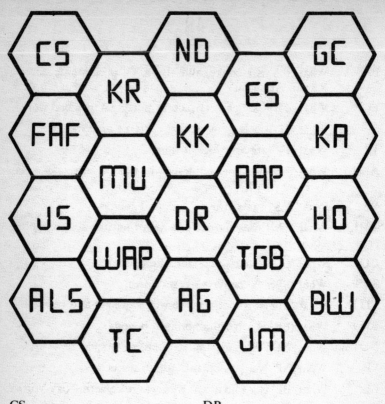

CS	_____	DR	_____
FAF	_____	AG	_____
JS	_____	ES	_____
ALS	_____	AAP	_____
KR	_____	TGB	_____
MU	_____	JM	_____
WAP	_____	GC	_____
TC	_____	KA	_____
ND	_____	HO	_____
KK	_____	BW	_____

49

CS: What 'CS' is part of a Sunday Paper?

FAF: What 'FAF' are plants and animals?

JS: What 'JS' are wealthy élite to be found in places like Saint Tropez?

ALS: What 'ALS' is the song sung to welcome in the New Year?

KR: What 'KR' is a large sum of money?

MU: What 'MU' is minor confusion and chaos where things get in a mess?

WAP: What 'WAP' was the epic by Leo Tolstoy?

TC: What 'TC' is a spicy Indian dish?

ND: What 'ND' was the plan for reconstruction laid down by President Roosevelt in the 1930s?

KK: What 'KK' was the footballer who left Newcastle United in 1984?

DR: What 'DR' played the main role in *Lady Sings The Blues*?

AG: What 'AG' is the Government's Law Officer?

ES: What 'ES' is a descendant of the Aga Khan who has recently started a newspaper?

AAP: What 'AAP' is Cockney rhyming slang for stairs?

TGB: What 'TGB' was a film from a book by L.P. Hartley?

JM: What 'JM' was a march of unemployed from Newcastle to London in the 1920s?

GC: What 'GC' wrote the *Canterbury Tales*?

KA: What 'KA' is reputed to have burnt the cakes?

HO: What 'HO' means to intercept?

BW: What 'BW' separates East from West Germany?

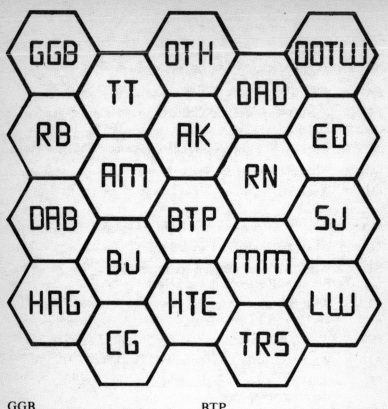

GGB	_____	BTP	_____
RB	_____	HTE	_____
DAB	_____	DAD	_____
HAG	_____	RN	_____
TT	_____	MM	_____
AM	_____	TRS	_____
BJ	_____	OOTW	_____
CG	_____	ED	_____
OTH	_____	SJ	_____
AK	_____	LW	_____

50

GGB: What 'GGB' is the bridge which spans San Francisco?

RB: What 'RB' was the World War 1 German flying ace?

DAB: What 'DAB' means to run away?

HAG: What 'HAG' were tempted by a gingerbread house?

TT: What 'TT' is nicknamed 'The Thunderer'?

AM: What 'AM' is the name sometimes given by students to their university or college?

BJ: What 'BJ' wrote *The Alchemist*?

CG: What 'CG' was once known for its vegetable market and is the location of the Opera House?

OTH: What 'OTH' means unprepared?

AK: What 'AK' is the tragic heroine in a famous novel by Tolstoy?

BTP: What 'BTP' sparked off the American War of Independence?

HTE: What 'HTE' was the King who dissolved the monasteries?

DAD: What 'DAD' is a game involving throwing stones onto water?

RN: What 'RN' was the American President brought down by the Watergate scandal?

MM: What 'MM' is a charwoman?

TRS: What 'TRS' were a famous R&R band in the '60s and '70s?

OOTW: What 'OOTW' means out of danger?

ED: What 'ED' means 'the golden land'?

SJ: What 'SJ' is a motorway interchange in Birmingham?

LW: What 'LW' is the leader of Solidarity in Poland?

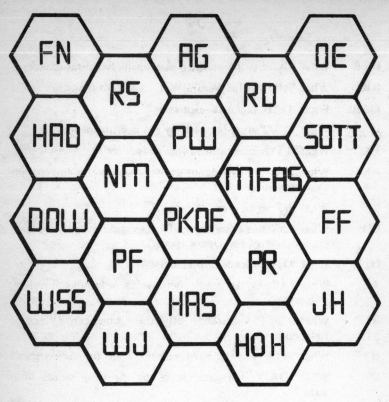

FN	————————	PKOF	————————
HAD	————————	HAS	————————
DOW	————————	RD	————————
WSS	————————	MFAS	————————
RS	————————	PR	————————
NM	————————	HOH	————————
PF	————————	OE	————————
WJ	————————	SOTT	————————
AG	————————	FF	————————
PW	————————	JH	————————

51

FN: What 'FN' was also known as 'The Lady of the Lamp'?

HAD: What 'HAD' means stranded?

DOW: What 'DOW' are mercenaries?

WSS: What 'WSS' is a famous Leonard Bernstein musical?

RS: What 'RS' is a well-known dictionary of synonyms?

NM: What 'NM' is a Greek singer, who had a chart success with 'Only Love'?

PF: What 'PF' is an old-fashioned type of high bicycle?

WJ: What 'WJ' is a garden shrub with yellow flowers which blooms late in the year?

AG: What 'AG' is the irascible cockney character portrayed by Warren Mitchell in *Till Death Us Do Part*?

PW: What 'PW' is a revolving disc to carry clay during moulding of earthenware vessels?

PKOF: What 'PKOF' means an awkward state of affairs?

HAS: What 'HAS' is the emblem on the national flag of the USSR?

RD: What 'RD' is the host of the TV programme *Question Time*?

MFAS: What 'MFAS' is the well-known play by Robert Bolt about Thomas More?

PR: What 'PR' is an electoral system supported by the SDP/Liberal Alliance?

HOH: What 'HOH' means rather deaf?

OE: What 'OE' is the train where murder took place, in a famous Agatha Christie story?

SOTT: What 'SOTT' is something said by accident, when meaning something else?

FF: What 'FF' are potato chips?

JH: What 'JH' is a musical instrument played between the teeth?

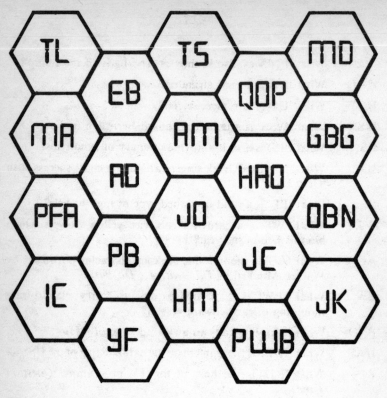

TL	_____	JO	_____
MA	_____	HM	_____
PFA	_____	QOP	_____
IC	_____	HAO	_____
EB	_____	JC	_____
AD	_____	PWB	_____
PB	_____	MD	_____
YF	_____	GBG	_____
TS	_____	OBN	_____
AM	_____	JK	_____

52

TL: What 'TL' is a popular show hosted by Esther Rantzen?

MA: What 'MA' are the warlike practices of Asia?

PFA: What 'PFA' means to subject to ridicule?

IC: What 'IC' divides the East from the West?

EB: What 'EB' catches the worm?

AD: What 'AD' wrote *The Count of Monte Cristo* and *The Three Musketeers*?

PB: What 'PB' is government stock with chances of cash prizes selected by ERNIE?

YF: What 'YF' is a tropical fever with jaundice?

TS: What 'TS' is a woman's matching cardigan and jumper?

AM: What 'AM' is an old building preserved under government control?

JO: What 'JO' wrote *Look Back In Anger*?

HM: What 'HM' is solid rock music?

QOP: What 'QOP' is a dessert made with breadcrumbs and meringue?

HAO: What 'HAO' means ugly and elderly?

JC: What 'JC' is a person who upsets you whilst trying to cheer you up?

PWB: What 'PWB' is President of South Africa?

MD: What 'MD' is a purple flower which blooms in autumn?

GBG: What 'GBG' should you beware of?

OBN: What 'OBN' is a supposed system of favouritism among ex-public schoolboys?

JK: What 'JK' wrote *Ode to a Nightingale*?

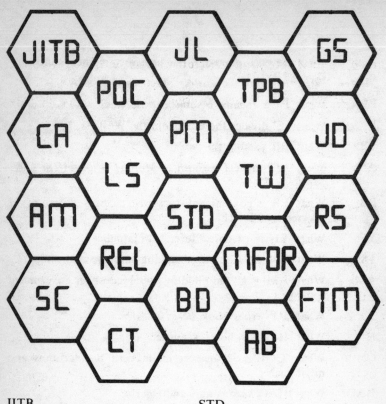

JITB	_____	STD	_____
CA	_____	BD	_____
AM	_____	TPB	_____
SC	_____	TW	_____
POC	_____	MFOR	_____
LS	_____	AB	_____
REL	_____	GS	_____
CT	_____	JD	_____
JL	_____	RS	_____
PM	_____	FTM	_____

53

JITB: What 'JITB' is a toy figure that springs out of a box when it is opened?

CA: What 'CA' is the malicious destruction of a person's reputation?

AM: What 'AM' is a fictional character who wrote a diary and had growing pains?

SC: What 'SC' is a place in London where orators can speak, free from arrest?

POC: What 'POC' is a place where a ship stops during its journey?

LS: What 'LS' is an item of news given prominence in a newspaper?

REL: What 'REL' was the General who commanded the Confederate Army during the American Civil War?

CT: What 'CT' is about to become a fixed link between Great Britain and France?

JL: What 'JL' is the malaise felt after a long aircraft flight?

PM: What 'PM' are gold, silver, platinum?

STD: What 'STD' means to take the average of two proposed amounts?

BD: What 'BD' is found at a fairground?

TPB: What 'TPB' is a popular indoor sport involving skittles?

TW: What 'TW' is a well-known TV interviewer?

MFOR: What 'MFOR' means profit for little or no trouble?

AB: What 'AB' played 'Strangers on the Shore'?

GS: What 'GS' was when British labour ceased work in 1926?

JD: What 'JD' stars with her husband in *A Fine Romance*?

RS: What 'RS' gathers no moss?

FTM: What 'FTM' means not to shirk the consequences?

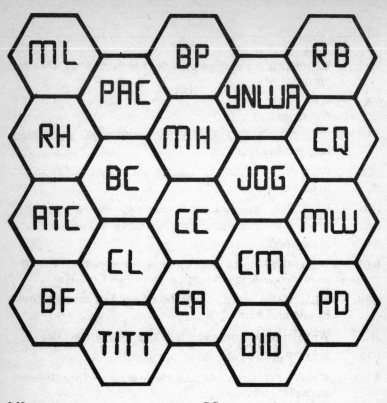

ML	_____	CC	_____
RH	_____	EA	_____
ATC	_____	YNWA	_____
BF	_____	JOG	_____
PAC	_____	CM	_____
BC	_____	DID	_____
CL	_____	RB	_____
TITT	_____	CQ	_____
BP	_____	MW	_____
MH	_____	PD	_____

54

ML: What 'ML' is a military government?

RH: What 'RH' robbed from the rich to give to the poor?

ATC: What 'ATC' guides planes into airports?

BF: What 'BF' is the TV personality who says 'Nice to see you . . . to see you nice'?

PAC: What 'PAC' means to be selective?

BC: What 'BC' is a well-known female novelist, who is related to Princess Diana?

CL: What 'CL' are worn instead of spectacles?

TITT: What 'TITT' means to admit defeat?

BP: What 'BP' is a small role in a play or a film?

MH: What 'MH' went to the cupboard to fetch her poor dog a bone?

CC: What 'CC' is a best selling novelist from the North of England who wrote books about Tilly Trotter?

EA: What 'EA' deals in buying and selling houses?

YNWA: What 'YNWA' was the song sung by The Crowd to raise money for the victims of the Bradford Fire Disaster?

JOG: What 'JOG' is at the extreme north of Scotland?

CM: What 'CM' is an economic and political association of nine European countries?

DID: What 'DID' is a radio show currently hosted by Michael Parkinson, formerly by Roy Plomley?

RB: What 'RB' is a much beloved cartoon character now immortalised by Paul McCartney?

CQ: What 'CQ' is a bed-covering used instead of blankets?

MW: What 'MW' is the Galaxy, or a chocolate bar?

PD: What 'PD' is Remembrance Sunday?

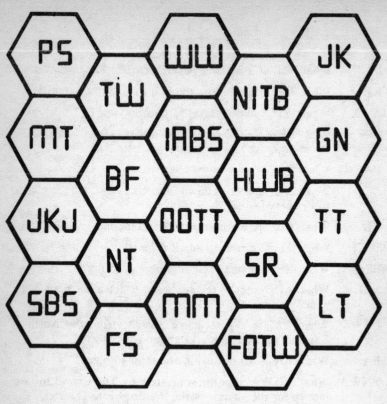

PS	_____	OOTT	_____
MT	_____	MM	_____
JKJ	_____	NITB	_____
SBS	_____	HWB	_____
TW	_____	SR	_____
BF	_____	FOTW	_____
NT	_____	JK	_____
FS	_____	GN	_____
WW	_____	TT	_____
IABS	_____	LT	_____

55

PS: What 'PS' is a building where electricity is generated for distribution?

MT: What 'MT' runs a hospice in Calcutta?

JKJ: What 'JKJ' wrote *Three Men in a Boat*?

SBS: What 'SBS' is a TV programme dealing with the arts, introduced by Melvyn Bragg?

TW: What 'TW' consists of countries like Asia, Africa etc?

BF: What 'BF' is a popular Spanish sport?

NT: What 'NT' is the private body for preserving historic or beautiful places?

FS: What 'FS' sang 'I'll do it my way'?

WW: What 'WW' is the high wall in Jerusalem said to stand on the site of Solomon's temple?

IABS: What 'IABS' means in a dream, absent-minded?

OOTT: What 'OOTT' is a Scottish order of knighthood?

MM: What 'MM' introduces *Mastermind*?

NITB: What 'NITB' means to destroy at an early stage of development?

HWB: What 'HWB' keeps your feet warm in bed?

SR: What 'SR' wrote *Midnight's Children*?

FOTW: What 'FOTW' is an unperceived observer?

JK: What 'JK' is an act of betrayal?

GN: What 'GN' is the annual steeplechase at Liverpool?

TT: What 'TT' was where convicted criminals were executed in London?

LT: What 'LT', former Doctor Barnardo's boy, achieved success with his novels *Virgin Soldiers* and *Tropic of Ruislip*?

Solution: Puzzle 1

AV: Amerigo Vespucci; EYM: Eligible Young Man; FW: *Finnegan's Wake*; HAD: Half A Dozen; IT: Income Tax; CTC: Cut The Cackle; GCG: General Charles Gordon; PT: Peeping Tom; KITR: Kiss In The Ring; NT: New Towns; LIW: Lie In Wait; JOS: Judgement of Solomon; OTS: On The Shelf; WH: Witch Hunt; VBP: Vote By Proxy; PW: Perkin Warbeck; WAG: Walker Art Gallery; MOTR: Master Of The Rolls; AGC: Advanced Gas Cooled; UMW: Under Milk Wood.

Solution: Puzzle 2

BNG: Butter Nut Grey; YOT: Your Own Trumpet; PV: Parma Violet; SC: Sacred Cow; CY: Cadmium Yellow; WB: Wright Brothers; RC: Rocking Chair; OAM: Old As Methuselah; JB: John Buchan; ITD: In The Drink; LRP: Last Resting Place; PIL: Put In Limbo; FYC: Fine Young Cannibals; NOS: Number One Seed; ER: Eightsome Reel; MM: Maid Marian; KD: Kiki Dee; FM: Field Marshal; HTS: Hands To Stations; GAD: Guys and Dolls.

Solution: Puzzle 3

OUAT: Once Upon A Time; COO: Climate Of Opinion; ITB: In The Belfry; GA: Gentleman's Agreement; AP: Alexander Pope; ND: Name Dropper; SAA: Sir Andrew Aguecheek; RAR: Right As Rain; JPS: Jean-Paul Sartre; UDF: Ulster Defence Force; HT: Henry Threadgill; POW: Prisoner Of War; WC: Winston Churchill; ATPM: *All The President's Men*; VDL: Van Diemen's Land; MD: Michaelmas Day; TOL: Tree Of Life; PKS: Professor Keith Simpson; LB: Louis Blériot; FSL: First Sea Lord.

Solution: Puzzle 4

ET: Elizabeth Taylor; CR: Cecil Rhodes; DS: Dog Star; IMF: International Monetary Fund; PIB: Puss In Boots; GB: Grizzly Bear; AGP: A Great Pyramid; ON: Old Nick; RFH: Royal Festival Hall; BOJ: Battle of Jutland; FOB: Full Of Beans; MR: Maurice Ravel; YOB: Your Own Back; KB: Keith Barron; NSD: Never Say Die; VOW: *Vicar of Wakefield*; WRH: William Randolph Hearst; AT: Arturo Toscanini; JW: Josiah Wedgwood; LRB: *Little Red Book*.

Solution: Puzzle 5

LOM: Leg Of Mutton; HF: Henry Ford; CTC: Cheek to Cheek; RP: Rolling Pin; GB: Goggle Box; IPC: International Publishing Corporation; JP: Juan Perón; NP: New Pin; OTWS: On The Wrong Side; AS: Andrés Segovia; FF: Flying Fish; BO: British Open (Golf Tournament); PR: Proportional Representation; ES: Epsom Salts; KCC: King's College Chapel; STD: Split The Difference; TPIR: *The Price Is Right*; MOO: Maid Of Orleans; DSS: Dead Sea Scrolls; UBR: University Boat Race.

Solution: Puzzle 6

AL: Abraham Lincoln; KR: Kind Regards; NB: Napoleon Bonaparte; TOTC: *Tale of Two Cities*; CR: Chief Rabbi; JB: Jelly Babies; PD: Punch Drunk; RM: Ready Made; BYU: Bob's Your Uncle; FM: Feeble Minded; LC: Lower Case; NN: *Nicholas Nickleby*; PM: Perpetual Motion; SH: Sherlock Holmes; TFLW: *The French Lieutenant's Woman*; YHA: Youth Hostels Association; CS: Cutty Sark; EP: End Product; GEM: Green Eyed Monster; RT: Rag Trade.

Solution: Puzzle 7

WP: William Pitt; SM: *Silas Marner* (by George Eliot); NF: New Forest; PM: Pipe Major; HG: Holy Grail; CT: Cautionary Tale; AH: Alfred Hitchcock; DL: David Livingstone; FAC: Fish And Chips; HP: Harold Pinter; LO: Leave Out; NPG: National Portrait Gallery; RR: Right Reverend; TOL: Tower Of London; WI: Women's Institute; DITR: Dig In The Ribs; BT: Ben Travers; EO: Eye Opener; GNR: Great North Road; JL: Joe Louis.

Solution: Puzzle 8

GB: Green Belt; AH: Aldous Huxley; KS: Karen Silkwood; SAS: Seven A Side; IV: In Vain; TC: Three Cheers; BSR: Bow Street Runners (before the police); OD: Occupational Disease; HC: Horse Chestnut; RW: Richard Wagner; YM: York Minster; VF: *Vanity Fair*; UTS: Up The Spout; VD: Valentine's Day; GD: Golden Delicious; LC: Lieutenant Colonel; COC: Contempt Of Court; EJ: Elton John; ITR: In The Red; BE: Break Even.

Solution: Puzzle 9

FS: Flag Ship; NMA: New Model Army; OT: Operating Theatre; RF: Rain Forest; UAD: Ups And Downs; TC: Trinity College; CJ: Clapham Junction; WE: White Elephant; UB: Unemployment Benefit; HJ: High Jump; WHC: World Heavyweight Championship; DH: Denis Healey; ITLD: In The Lion's Den; KL: King Lear; PD: Porton Down; YL: Yule Log; MC: Michael Crawford; SE: *Starlight Express*; GMC: General Medical Council; LW: Left Wing.

Solution: Puzzle 10

FP: Floyd Paterson; KH: Katherine Hepburn; WS: Whited Sepulchre; NWT: North-West Territories; AM: Abel Magwitch; LTT: Little Tommy Tucker; GP: Great Plague; PA: Psycho Analysis; MS: Moral Support; YC: Yellow Card; HS: Hydrogen Sulphide; RVW: Ralph Vaughan Williams; TH: The Hebrides; BS: Bram Stoker; DED: Dutch Elm Disease; FL: Filthy Lucre; IB: Ian Botham; VQ: Vexed Question; COA: Coat Of Arms; GTF: God The Father.

Solution: Puzzle 11

KW: Kurt Weill; RH: Rush Hour; ACM: Air Chief Marshal; DI: Dry Ice; SC: Samuel Cunard; YH: Yellow Hammer; FPN: Five Pound Note; BK: Butterfly Kiss; ML: *Modern Love*; TBO: *The Beggar's Opera*; IR: Insect Repellent; WW: William Wallace; CP: Carrier Pigeon; KTE: Kon Tiki Expedition; OC: Off Colour; GBS: George Bernard Shaw; PLS: Packed Like Sardines; EL: Edward Lear; LP: Lester Piggott; BNF: British Nuclear Fuels.

Solution: Puzzle 12

BM: Bain Marie; JC: Joseph Conrad; MA: Mark Antony; OF: Old Flame; TIA: The Idle Apprentice; AT: Acquired Taste; CD: Christian Dior; FC: Forbidden City; ITT: Ivan The Terrible; LG: Liqueur Glass; RE: Roman Empire; WAM: Ways And Means; DH: Dotheboys Hall; GA: Godwin Austen; KAK: Kith And Kin; SG: Strangers Gallery; EOE: Essays Of Elia; NW: New World; CO: Crude Oil; FF: Forbidden Fruit.

Solution: Puzzle 13

EV: Escape Velocity; GH: Gustav Holst; OM: Old Maid; ROI: Republic Of Ireland; AP: Action Painting; CDL: Coeur De Lion; IB: Ironing Board; DE: Duke Ellington; KT: Kill Time; ST: Spencer Tracy; WW: Who's Who; BHA: Big-Hearted Arthur (Askey); FS: Flying Saucer; JT: Jethro Tull; MC: Mexico City; THD: The Hundred Days; VB: Vampire Bat; CB: Cilla Black; GL: Gresham's Law; AG: Alec Guinness.

Solution: Puzzle 14

BH: By Hand; JN: Julius Nyerere; LM: Lawn Mower; TNN: The Naughty Nineties; DE: Dick Emery; FFT: Food For Thought; PR: Princess Royal; TTT: The Thomson Twins; AD: Artful Dodger; CO: Cast Off; ES: Earth Science; HOH: Hard Of Hearing; LBIA: *Look Back In Anger*; VC: Vacuum Cleaner; DC: Dutch Courage; FL: Franz Liszt; IB: Iron Bridge; TLK: *The Lady Killers*; WC: William Caxton; GM: German Measles.

Solution: Puzzle 15

AF: April Fool; GP: Green Paper; MOG: Massacre Of Glencoe; RW: Robert Walpole; TQE: Turn Queen's Evidence; CC: China Clay; FFF: Full Fathom Five; KP: Khyber Pass; NN: Nizhni Novgorod; SM: Shirley MacLaine; VG: Vocational Guidance; BB: Baffin Bay; DV: Deo Volente; HK: Helmut Kohl; LSD: Labour Saving Device; RM: Ramsay MacDonald; CK: Charles Kingsley; EH: Electric Hare; IM: Indian Mutiny; JK: Jonathan King.

Solution: Puzzle 16

BB: Behind Bars; EKN: Eine Kleine Nachtmusik; VV: Vice Versa; AWB: Anthony Wedgewood Benn; JC: Juan Carlos; LM: Lee Marvin; TBM: Three Blind Mice; OA: Oswaldo Ardiles; MHR: Many Happy Returns; RC: Remote Control; UTC: *Uncle Tom's Cabin*; EE: Edward Elgar; FK: Fort Knox; HF: Ham Fisted; DS: Dewey System; NM: Narrow Minded; WM: William Morris; CC: Captain Cook; EAI: *Ebony And Ivory*; GF: Golden Flute.

Solution: Puzzle 17

ES: Edith Sitwell; IP: Itching Palm; MK: *Mein Kampf*; UIA: Up In Arms; BA: Bloody Assizes; TGG: *The Great Gatsby*; DAH: Down At Heel; SP: Samuel Pepys; HH: Hitch Hike; JS: January Sales; CW: Christopher Wren; WO: Wild Oats; DB: Dead Body; FM: Foster Mother; HS: Holy Sepulchre; LOTF: *Lord Of The Flies*; MY: Musical Youth; SOL: Statue Of Liberty; UD: Ugly Duckling; AN: Arabian Nights.

Solution: Puzzle 18

FP: Funeral Pyre; HM: Henrietta Maria; ADL: A Dog's Life; DS: Dmitri Shostakovich; IVV: In Vino Veritas; NG: Natural Gas; TR: Third Reich; WB: Warren Beatty; CN: Cleopatra's Needle; EL: Ewe Lamb; JOA: Joan Of Arc; PG: Persian Gulf; RAC: Rich As Croesus; VP: Vantage Point; BF: Benjamin Franklin; DBM: Death By Misadventure; GH: Golden Handshake; ML: Maple Leaf; OTT: On Tip Toe; TH: Trojan Horse.

Solution: Puzzle 19

BD: Bone Dry; FF: Free Fall; IAH: In A Handbag; MR: Marty Robins; POM: Presence Of Mind; TCH: Three Cornered Hat; AD: Alfred Dreyfus; LJG: Lady Jane Grey; SA: Saudi Arabia; NS: Norway Spruce; RM: Reverend Mother; UTF: *Under Two Flags*; JA: Jenny Agutter; FRB: Forth Road Bridge; CB: Collar Bone; GB: Geoffrey Boycott; IN: Isaac Newton; MHT: Mad Hatter's Teaparty; OC: Oliver Cromwell; SK: South Korea.

Solution: Puzzle 20

NO: New Orleans; SG: Stained Glass; VOI: Viceroy Of India; BMA: British Medical Association; DK: Diane Keaton; HJ: Hacking Jacket; WA: White Ants; CAV: Chapter And Verse; FBN: Fly By Night; IW: Icknield Way; TTP: Take The Pledge; EH: Emmylou Harris; GSOE: Greatest Show On Earth; LB: *La Bohème*; NL: Northern Lights; RM: Royal Mint; VL: Vladimir Lenin; HAD: High And Dry; MLK: Martin Luther King; OY: *Only You*.

Solution: Puzzle 21

STW: Save The Whale; AP: Alexander Pope; SAA: Sergeant At Arms; MH: Make Hay; RDN: Robert De Niro; SWB: South Wales Borderers; WW: William Wordsworth; PC: Parmesan Cheese; BA: Barbary Ape; MAS: Marks And Spencer; NA: Neil Armstrong; HDH: *Hi De Hi*; MC: Magna Carta; RM: Rupert Murdoch; CP: Cheese Plant; SB: Starboard Bow; TC: Terence Conran; CP: Cinque Ports; HF: Hang Fire; CH: Chiltern Hundreds.

Solution: Puzzle 22

AEH: Alfred Edward Houseman; LM: Lake Maggiore; UK: United Kingdom; CC: Crown Courts; FZ: Franco Zefferelli; JG: John Glenn; SOF: Society Of Friends; UP: Under Par; BH: Buddy Holly; DAAB: Daft As A Brush; GT: Globe Trotter; IP: Isaac Pitman; MG: Mrs Gaskell; OOW: Out Of Water; TAJ: Tom And Jerry; WL: White Light; CR: Cresta Run; GO: George Orwell; NE: Nest Egg; MQOS: Mary Queen Of Scots.

Solution: Puzzle 23

CC: Capacity Crowd; AB: Anton Bruckner; TR: Tudor Rose; FYN: Feather Your Nest; MC: Monte Carlo; OG: Old Glory; SB: Samuel Beckett; CA: Combination Act; ETB: Et Tu, Brute; GOG: Garden Of Gethsemane; NML: No Man's Land; PP: *Pickwick Papers*; RIP: Rod In Pickle; TA: Total Abstainer; BR: Broken Reed; DOW: Duke Of Wellington; FL: First Lady; HMSV: Her Majesty's Ship Victory; JS: Jonathan Swift; PH: Procol Harum.

Solution: Puzzle 24

AOC: Anne Of Cleves; BD: Barn Dance; CBAH: Charity Begins At Home; DB: Dogger Bank; EB: Eubi Blake; FE: Field Events; GF: Glass Fibre; HOH: Holy Of Holies; JW: John Wyndham; IF: Irresistible Force; LB: Lonsdale Belt; MS: Moonlight Sonata; JH: John Hawkins; OL: Ohm's Law; PL: *Paradise Lost*; RHM: Right Hand Man; SD: State Department; TH: Trinity House; WM: Walrus Moustache; BAC: Box And Cox.

Solution: Puzzle 25

RS: Red Shift; PL: Philip Larkin; AS: Alexei Sayle; CPBS: Cast Pearls Before Swine; FB: Flying Bombs; BS: Bruce Springsteen; CAD: Cats And Dogs; TDF: Tierra Del Fuego; HN: Half Nelson; LM: Liza Minnelli; PCA: Parliamentary Commissioner Administration; RS: Red Sky; AWP: *Auf Wiedersehen Pet*; MW: Malt Whisky; AK: Alfred Krupp; RE: Royal Engineers; CF: Chequered Flag; FT: Family Tree; HYW: Hundred Years' War; PS: Pulling Strings.

Solution: Puzzle 26

LLBS: *Late Late Breakfast Show*; GW: Guerilla Warfare; JOAT: Jack Of All Trades; LE: Land's End; PTQ: Pop The Question; SS: Sixth Sense; WD: *Watership Down*; OTBT: Off The Beaten Track; JK: Jack Kerouac; LOH: Lap Of Honour; KKK: Ku Klux Klan; SIT: Stitch In Time; LQ: Latin Quarter; JR: Jolly Roger; FHTM: From Hand To Mouth; AHAL: As Happy As Larry; TOTD: *Tess Of The D'Urbervilles*; PC: Phil Collins; JW: Jehovah's Witnesses; OFT: Old Father Thames.

Solution: Puzzle 27

JAH: Jekyll And Hyde; GG: *Goodbye Girl*; AV: Authorised Version; HG: Holy Ghost; SCD: Saint Crispin's Day; BO: Bill Oddie; DS: Domestic Science; FD: Flag Down; LBH: Learn By Heart; MD: *Moby Dick*; PS: Palm Sunday; CG: Chlorine Gas; BD: Bob Dylan; DKJP: D'ye Ken John Peel; HT: Half Time; LOA: Little Orphan Annie; OW: Oscar Wilde; SS: Secret Service; BM: Benito Mussolini; MS: Muriel Spark.

Solution: Puzzle 28

TRD: To Render Down; HF: Harvest Festival; SC: Select Committee; AP: Al Pacino; DTTW: Dead To The World; TBWS: To Blind With Science; GR: Ginger Rogers; KOOC: Keep One's Own Counsel; DD: Duran Duran; PA: Political Asylum; JC: Jimmy Carter; HTR: Hit The Roof; BITH: Bird In The Hand; LS: Lion's Share; SAD: Stand And Deliver; OU: Open University; BOS: Barber Of Seville; DC: Dirt Cheap; FC: Fastnet Cup; PL: Poet Laureate.

Solution: Puzzle 29

ITD: In The Doldrums; TG: True Grit; GMT: Greenwich Mean Time; COTE: Chancellor Of The Exchequer; KA: Kingsley Amis; PP: Passion Play; TMC: Too Many Cooks; TRL: Thin Red Line; GM: Gustav Mahler; SG: South Georgia; VV: Viva Voce; BIW: Barkis Is Willing; SF: Sinn Fein; ROT: Rule Of Thumb; BV: Bon Voyage; IC: In Camera; FT: *Fawlty Towers*; DOW: Duke Of Wellington; DH: Dead Heat; MHLS: More Haste Less Speed.

Solution: Puzzle 30

RIB: Romans In Britain; GOB: Go One Better; DS: Dire Straits; POW: Prince Of Wales; RH: Roy Hattersley; HIO: Hit It Off; CB: Collective Bargaining; NSA: No Strings Attached; ER: *Educating Rita*; WAG: Wig And Gown; MOV: *Merchant Of Venice*; BOTB: Battle Of The Bulge; SW: Salem Witchhunt; MM: Miss Marple; HC: Hobson's Choice; BB: Botany Bay; GOW: Grapes Of Wrath; FOS: Fleet Of Sail; ASIB: *A Star Is Born*; GKW: Good King Wenceslas.

Solution: Puzzle 31

MBEM: Make Both Ends Meet; SS: Sylvester Stallone; PL: Picket Line; HF: Hold Forth; BAT: Black And Tans; EC: Every Cloud; OGP: *On Golden Pond*; BR: Black Rod; FOG: Flock Of Geese; GAS: Gilbert And Sullivan; RFAF: Ride For A Fall; BPC: Bonny Prince Charlie; JB: Josephine Baker; ALE: At Loose Ends; GF: Garret Fitzgerald; OW: Orson Welles; IF: Idée Fixe; JOTP: Justice Of The Peace; KC: Keep Cool; RM: Royal Marines.

Solution: Puzzle 32

DQ: *Don Quixote*; PM: Peach Melba; BM: Black Market; GA: Grey Area; TDH: *The Deer Hunter*; LAE: Lend An Ear; EMF: E.M. Forster; SAF: San Andreas Fault; VSOP: Very Superior Old Pale; ITP: In The Picture; BB: Black Box; LITD: Leap In The Dark; RK: Rudyard Kipling; BOT: Battle Of Trafalgar; JT: Jeremy Thorpe; POC: Pack Of Cards; CI: Cave In; SUA: Stratford Upon Avon; NW: Neighbourhood Watch; GAWI: Get Away With It.

Solution: Puzzle 33

BS: Black Sheep; LL: Laurie Lee; SW: *Star Wars*; QOH: Queen Of Hearts; GS: Granny Smith; HOT: Helen Of Troy; CM: Christopher Marlowe; LON: Land Of Nod; PE: Paul Eddington; CS: Captain Scott; STRS: Set The Record Straight; CP: Carrier Pigeon; HU: Hard Up; SITD: Shot In The Dark; HM: Harold MacMillan; MW: Mary Wilson; BR: *Brideshead Revisited*; PA: Princess Anne; YG: Yuri Gagarin; JB: Juliet Bravo.

Solution: Puzzle 34

HOTC: Haul Over The Coals; NDP: Nom De Plume; ISO: In Spite Of; ML: Mona Lisa; EM: Elgin Marbles; SP: Scafell Pike; LH: Larry Hagman; WT: William Tell; ITP: In The Pink; TGH: Ten Gallon Hat; WC: Winston Churchill; PP: Peter Pan; RA: Red Admiral; AS: Anwar Sadat; HAB: Hot And Bothered; FAA: Flanagan And Allen; AF: Alexander Fleming; SSB: South Sea Bubble; WT: Wat Tyler; HC: Horse Chestnut.

Solution: Puzzle 35

CC: Common Cold; IO: Indian Ocean; MR: Monmouth Rebellion; HK: Henry Kissinger; BS: Brussels Sprouts; DF: Dry Fly; BD: Bernadette Devlin; MAF: Make A Face; PO: Petty Officer; SITB: Stab In The Back; BC: Bob Champion; QS: Quantity Surveyor; IMC: In Mint Condition; SUL: Stiff Upper Lip; TF: Terra Firma; BG: Bob Geldof; NH: Natural History; GS: Good Samaritan; HB: Hywell Bennett; SJ: Scott Joplin.

Solution: Puzzle 36

TFL: Take French Leave; SAS: Safe And Sound; PV: Pyrrhic Victory; RLS: Robert Louis Stevenson; MT: Madame Tussauds; SOL: Sooner Or Later; PS: Percy Shelley; FAF: Forgive And Forget; EP: Eva Perón; DI: Devil's Island; FB: Fast Breeder; OC: Operation Countryman; BP: Beatrix Potter; LT: Legal Tender; WH: *Wuthering Heights*; NK: Ned Kelly; PP: *Pink Panther*; GC: George Cross; ERB: Edgar Rice Burroughs; FC: Fatted Calf.

Solution: Puzzle 37

GP: Guinea Pig; ACD: Arthur Conan Doyle; PU: Punch Up; MC: Morse Code; SG: Super Grass; CR: Cecil Rhodes; TE: Timothy Evans; RB: Robert Browning; HH: Heinrich Himmler; PP: Pablo Picasso; SWR: Sir Walter Raleigh; EP: Exhaust Pipe; CS: Chromatic Scale; SE: Stand Easy; POP: Plaster Of Paris; LH: Len Hutton; PT: Percy Thrower; GF: Grand Finale; TOY: *Testament Of Youth*; SFS: Start From Scratch.

Solution: Puzzle 38

RDB: R.D. Blackmore; HW: Heavy Water; PB: Push Bike; SMS: Sir Malcolm Sargent; EI: Emerald Isle; RVW: Rip Van Winkle; TS: Tasman Sea; RN: Rudolf Nureyev; ML: Martin Luther; VH: Victor Hugo; TPD: The Peak District; IN: Isaac Newton; JS: John Steinbeck; ET: Eiffel Tower; SP: Salisbury Plain; PH: Pearl Harbor; HH: Heartbreak Hotel; AS: Alexander Solzhenitsyn; WTC: William The Conqueror; RBP: Robert Baden Powell.

Solution: Puzzle 39

ST: Shaw Taylor; NO: New Orleans; GS: Georges Simenon; HB: Humming Bird; AS: After Sun; POJ: Patience Of Job; BAR: Beat A Retreat; SJB: Sir John Betjeman; SFD: Sir Francis Drake; MU: Manchester United; BC: British Columbia; TSL: The Southern Lights; WS: Wormwood Scrubs; SJ: Samuel Johnson; PPTP: Put Pen To Paper; MK: Mount Kilimanjaro; SA: Stone Age; GD: Gun Dog; STC: Send To Coventry; LHO: Lee Harvey Oswald.

Solution: Puzzle 40

SP: Scarlet Pimpernel; IGF: In Good Faith; TGE: *The Great Escape*; ROH: Roll Of Honour; MN: Magnetic North; JK: Jack Ketch; SC: Saint Christopher; HCA: Hans Christian Andersen; GB: *General Belgrano*; HC: Halley's Comet; MG: Machine Gun; RW: Rainbow Warrior; BAM: Burgess And Maclean; TOF: *The Odessa File*; AS: Andrew Sachs; POW: Pull One's Weight; KH: Kitty Hawk; SS: Silly Season; FC: Fidel Castro; AAM: A.A. Milne.

Solution: Puzzle 41

PIK: Payment In Kind; SC: Suez Canal; ITDH: In The Dog House; EP: Elysée Palace; BAF: Blow A Fuse; LHH: Lord Haw Haw; PAQ: Pick A Quarrel; BM: Baader Meinhof; WF: Wells Fargo; YO: Yoko Ono; NC: Neville Chamberlain; CU: Call Up; LR: Leonard Rossiter; RP: Regents Park; ONJ: Olivia Newton John; YA: Yasser Arafat; GBR: Great Barrier Reef; CM: Custom Made; OOB: Out Of Bounds; DN: Deadly Nightshade.

Solution: Puzzle 42

PG: Peter Gabriel; AN: Alfred Nobel; BM: Bernard Montgomery; SAG: Simon And Garfunkel; AA: *'Allo 'Allo*; RB: Ronnie Barker; GF: Girl Friday; BATB: Beat About The Bush; MA: Marie Antoinette; OP: *Ordinary People*; CT: Coal Tar; BO: Benedictine Order; TWM: Three Wise Men; DD: Dry Dock; DHL: D.H. Lawrence; AR: Access Road; CF: Citrus Fruit; KD: Kettle Drum; RC: Raymond Chandler; AH: Albert Hall.

Solution: Puzzle 43

GB: Green Berets; BB: Big Ben; MS: *Morning Star*; LR: Lloyds Register; BOE: Bank Of England; TW: Terry Waite; DG: Double Glazing; CAW: Curds And Whey; RG: Robert Graves; FL: Fast Lane; AA: Adam's Ale; CH: Combine Harvester; BH: Brand's Hatch; GH: Gift Horse; TM: *The Mousetrap*; TAD: Torvill And Dean; BH: Black Hole; MITC: *Murder In The Cathedral*; RH: Rudolph Hess; IM: Iron Maiden.

Solution: Puzzle 44

DB: Dogger Bank; RM: Rolling Mill; HSB: *Hill Street Blues*; HF: Harrison Ford; IOM: Isle Of Man; MC: Malcolm Campbell; ASD: All Saint's Day; TH: Ted Hughes; HWH: Half Way House; TL: Turnip Lantern; PP: Public Purse; BT: Bermuda Triangle; RCS: Rose Coloured Spectacles; LS: Least Said; MV: Mount Vesuvius; LDV: Leonardo Da Vinci; GT: Good Turn; SW: Shirley Williams; BO: Bath Oliver; CB: Carte Blanche.

Solution: Puzzle 45

LV: Lake Victoria; TTI: *The Towering Inferno*; DE: Double Entendre; TOTS: *Turn Of The Screw*; OOD: Out Of Doors; CM: Calendar Month; SD: Steve Davies; BM: British Museum; CB: Caged Bird; OTS: On The Shelf; JA: Julie Andrews; POC: Piece Of Cake; JC: Johnny Cash; MOC: Man Of Calibre; BTB: Bring To Book; PL: Party Line; GW: Great War; NT: Nuremberg Trials; RF: Roaring Forties; DOO: Difference Of Opinion.

Solution: Puzzle 46

DITM: Down In The Mouth; EC: Eric Clapton; DJL: Davy Jones' Locker; WA: Westminster Abbey; ES: Evening Star; FGTH: Frankie Goes To Hollywood; GG: Graham Greene; MH: March Hare; MM: *Mad Max*; OTC: Off The Cuff; AF: Antonia Fraser; BB: Billy Bunter; PE: Personal Effects; IR: Industrial Revolution; TH: Tony Hancock; SS: Swan Song; JDV: Joie De Vivre; OD: Open Day; CB: Colorado Beetle; PS: Pamela Stephenson.

Solution: Puzzle 47

OAB: One Armed Bandit; RC: Remote Control; TMOV: *The Merchant Of Venice*; SA: Side Arms; TMB: The Marx Brothers; RR: Rob Roy; AF: Asian Flu; OTD: On The Dot; AW: Ash Wednesday; SP: Samuel Pepys; DB: David Bowie; HC: Howard Carter; MH: More Haste; SS: Sandie Shaw; FI: Fresian Islands; BOJ: Battle Of Jutland; KVK: *Kramer Vs. Kramer*; KM: Karl Marx; SJ: Spinning Jenny; AA: Aberdeen Angus.

Solution: Puzzle 48

BA: Black Adder; TCP: The Caring Professions; JJ: Jumbo Jet; TZ: The Zodiac; AM: Amadeus Mozart; YS: *Yellow Submarine*; TMI: Three Mile Island; GC: Grandfather Clock; SBS: Special Boat Service; TITH: Toad In The Hole; BR: Blaydon Races; NOTW: *News Of The World*; SP: Spider Plant; BF: Bryan Ferry; TS: Tall Story; LR: Lone Ranger; POC: Pair Of Compasses; WP: Wood Pigeon; TOTU: Tales Of The Unexpected; WG: Wool Gathering.

Solution: Puzzle 49

CS: Colour Supplement; FAF: Flora And Fauna; JS: Jet Set; ALS: Auld Lang Syne; KR: King's Ransom; MU: Mix Up; WAP: *War And Peace*; TC: Tandoori Chicken; ND: New Deal; KK: Kevin Keegan; DR: Diana Ross; AG: Attorney General; ES: Eddie Shah; AAP: Apples And Pears; TGB: *The Go Between*; JM: Jarrow March; GC: Geoffrey Chaucer; KA: King Alfred; HO: Head Off; BW: Berlin Wall.

Solution: Puzzle 50

GGB: Golden Gate Bridge; RB: Red Baron; DAB: Do A Bunk; HAG: Hansel And Gretel; TT: The Times; AM: Alma Mater; BJ: Ben Jonson; CG: Covent Garden; OTH: On The Hop; AK: Anna Karenina; BTP: Boston Tea Party; HTE: Henry The Eighth; DAD: Ducks And Drakes; RN: Richard Nixon; MM: Mrs Mop; TRS: The Rolling Stones; OOTW: Out Of The Wood; ED: El Dorado; SJ: Spaghetti Junction; LW: Lech Walesa.

Solution: Puzzle 51

FN: Florence Nightingale; HAD: High And Dry; DOW: Dogs Of War; WSS: *West Side Story*; RS: *Roget's Thesaurus*; NM: Nana Mouskouri; PF: Penny Farthing; WJ: Winter Jasmine; AG: Alf Garnett; PW: Potter's Wheel; PKOF: Pretty Kettle Of Fish; HAS: Hammer And Sickle; RD: Robin Day; MFAS: *Man For All Seasons*; PR: Proportional Representation; HOH: Hard Of Hearing; OE: Orient Express; SOTT: Slip Of The Tongue; FF: French Fries; JH: Jew's Harp.

Solution: Puzzle 52

TL: *That's Life*; MA: Martial Arts; PFA: Poke Fun At; IC: Iron Curtain; EB: Early Bird; AD: Alexander Dumas; PB: Premium Bond; YF: Yellow Fever; TS: Twin Set; AM: Ancient Monument; JO: John Osborne; HM: Heavy Metal; QOP: Queen Of Puddings; HAO: Haggard And Old; JC: Job's Comforter; PWB: P.W. Botha; MD: Michaelmas Daisy; GBG: Greeks Bearing Gifts; OBN: Old Boy Network; JK: John Keats.

Solution: Puzzle 53

JITB: Jack In The Box; CA: Character Assassination; AM: Adrian Mole; SC: Speakers' Corner; POC: Port Of Call; LS: Lead Story; REL: Robert E. Lee; CT: Channel Tunnel; JL: Jet Lag; PM: Precious Metals; STD: Split The Difference; BD: Big Dipper; TPB: Ten Pin Bowling; TW: Terry Wogan; MFOR: Money For Old Rope; AB: Acker Bilk; GS: General Strike; JD: Judi Dench; RS: Rolling Stone; FTM: Face The Music.

Solution: Puzzle 54

ML: Martial Law; RH: Robin Hood; ATC: Air Traffic Controller; BF: Bruce Forsyth; PAC: Pick And Choose; BC: Barbara Cartland; CL: Contact Lenses; TITT: Throw In The Towel; BP: Bit Part; MH: Mother Hubbard; CC: Catherine Cookson; EA: Estate Agent; YNWA: You'll Never Walk Alone; JOG: John O'Groats; CM: Common Market; DID: *Desert Island Discs*; RB: Rupert Bear; CQ: Continental Quilt; MW: Milky Way; PD: Poppy Day.

Solution: Puzzle 55

PS: Power Station; MT: Mother Teresa; JKJ: Jerome K. Jerome; SBS: *South Bank Show*; TW: Third World; BF: Bull Fighting; NT: National Trust; FS: Frank Sinatra; WW: Wailing Wall; IABS: In A Brown Study; OOTT: Order Of The Thistle; MM: Magnus Magnussen; NITB: Nip In The Bud; HWB: Hot Water Bottle; SR: Salman Rushdie; FOTW: Fly On The Wall; JK: Judas Kiss; GN: Grand National; TT: Tyburn Tree; LT: Leslie Thomas.

A selection of bestsellers from SPHERE

FICTION

BEACHES	Iris Rainer Dart	£2.95 ☐
RAINBOW SOLDIERS	Walter Winward	£3.50 ☐
FAMILY ALBUM	Danielle Steel	£2.95 ☐
SEVEN STEPS TO TREASON	Michael Hartland	£2.50 ☐

FILM AND TV TIE-IN

9$^1/_2$ WEEKS	Elizabeth McNeil	£1.95 ☐
BOON	Anthony Masters	£2.50 ☐
AUF WIEDERSEHEN PET 2	Fred Taylor	£2.75 ☐
LADY JANE	Anthony Smith	£1.95 ☐

NON-FICTION

THE FALL OF SAIGON	David Butler	£3.95 ☐
LET'S FACE IT	Christine Piff	£2.50 ☐
LIVING WITH DOGS	Sheila Hocken	£3.50 ☐
HOW TO SHAPE UP YOUR MAN	Catherine & Neil Mackwood	£2.95 ☐

All Sphere books are available at your local bookshop or newsagent, or can be ordered direct from the publisher. Just tick the titles you want and fill in the form below.

Name _____

Address _____

_____

Write to Sphere Books, Cash Sales Department, P.O. Box 11, Falmouth, Cornwall TR10 9EN.

Please enclose cheque or postal order to the value of the cover price plus:

UK: 55p for the first book, 22p for the second and 14p per copy for each additional book ordered to a maximum charge of £1.75.

OVERSEAS: £1.00 for the first book and 25p for each additional book.

BFPO & EIRE: 55p for the first book, 22p for the second book plus 14p per copy for the next 7 books, thereafter 8p per book.

Sphere Books reserve the right to show new retail prices on covers which may differ from those previously advertised in the text or elsewhere, and to increase postal rates in accordance with the PO.